BEFORE THE BLIND

Facts and Sources from the:

🍂 TORAH, PROPHETS, SCRIPTURES 🍂

🍂 MISHNAH, TALMUD, GEONIM 🍂

🍂 RISHONIM & ACHRONIM 🍂

Related to our attitude and
conduct toward **ANIMALS**

Presenting facts and bringing sources from
THE TORAH AND OUR SAGES
in full and without modification

"DO NOT PLACE A STUMBLING BLOCK

BEFORE THE BLIND" (Vayikra 19:14)

AF446884

Asa Keisar
Before the Blind

All rights reserved
Copyright © 2024 by Asa Keisar

No part of this publication may be reproduced, distributed, or transmitted in any form or by any means, including photocopying, recording, or other electronic or mechanical methods, without the prior written permission of the publisher, except in the case of brief quotations embodied in critical reviews and certain other noncommercial uses permitted by copyright law.

Published by Spines Publishing Platform
ISBN: 979-8-89383-695-0

Blessing Page

It is
known
that
**repairing the world
and settling it**
is achieved by
guiding people
and providing them
with good advice.

(Sefer HaChinuch, commandment 232)

Translated from Hebrew by: **Rabbi Donn (Shabtai) Gross**

Verses from the Bible are also been taken from www.sefaria.com

from this two Resourses:

1. Tanakh: The Holy Scriptures (2006). www.jps.org

2. Metsudah Chumash. Metsudah Publications (2009)

Translation edited by: **Batzion Shlomi**

ORder and Layout by: **Uriya Lev Sameach**

Published in 5783 / 2022

First published in Hebrew: 5778 / 2018

Please Join Us

in helping to spread the word
and become our partner in being a light
to all of Israel and the world at large.

To donate, please go to:
https://AsaKeisar.com/en/donate/
or send an e-mail to:
asakeisar@gmail.com

With blessings of peace,
Asa Keisar

The B∞K
"BEFORE THE BLIND"

has been written to benefit the public, and it is distributed *FOR FREE.* **IN ISRAEL**

It is a MITZVAH to disseminate it and permission is granted to copy it, but not for profit.

THE PRESIDENT
JERUSALEM, 26 HESHVAN, 5778
November 15, 2017

To: ASA KEISAR

Dear ASA,

I am happily obliged to thank you for your book, **"BEFORE THE BLIND"**, which allowed me to become familiar with your work as a supporter and promoter of Veganism and animal rights in the Orthodox and Haredi Judaism spheres. It is clear that you are doing ground breaking and courageous work, nothing less than a true revolution.

I have never forgotten the life changing experience I had as a child when my beloved dog Stefan was taken into quarantine in the dog pound, which was right near a slaughterhouse in Jerusalem. Every evening I clearly heard the sounds and saw the fear in the helpless animals' eyes. I always loved animals, but from that day on I became a Vegetarian and I believe with all of my heart that animals have the right to live as creatures in their own right and not only to serve man.

Sharing the message with people as you do as a grassroots movement is complex and multilayered and yet the number of Vegetarians and Vegans in the world has been steadily increasing over the years and Israel is one of the world leaders in the percentage of Vegetarian and Vegan residents. The references to our Biblical sources, the engaging of the warm Jewish heart and the imparting of the knowledge that Veganism is not only a moral imperative but also a Jewish imperative, is undoubtedly a significant step in the direction of the awaited and desired change.

I am very hopeful that over the next few years more and more people will join your righteous journey, and that soon the Jewish people and the State of Israel will be a light among the Nations of the world and be proud, among other things, of the compassionate and conscientious policies towards animals.

I AM A VEGETARIAN!

Respectfully and appreciatively yours,

REUVEN (RUBY) RIVLIN
JERUSALEM

APPROBATION for the book
"BEFORE THE BLIND" by R' ASA KEISAR

IT is my honor to congratulate R' Asa Keisar on the publication of his important book, which collates the Jewish sources concerning THE TORAH's approach towards animal life, and clarifies the grave transgressions involved in the current animal food industry, especially the cruelty to animals in the rearing of livestock and fowl, their transportation and treatment etc., which today involve brutality on a scale never known before.

In addition to these transgressions, we should also note the harm that such products cause to those who consume them, as they are full of hormones and antibiotics, which are pumped into the animals in the process of rearing them for slaughter, in violation of the injunction to take care of our health and distance ourselves from any harm (see RAMBAM, YAD HAHAZAKAH, HILKHOT ROTZE'ACH 11:4.)

And regarding the prohibition of "BAL TASHCHIT" against wastage, note must be made of the enormous waste of natural resources in animal food production, including water, land and grain etc. in the rearing of animals for slaughter -

resources that could provide plant food for more than forty times the amount of people, while more than thirty thousand children in the world die of hunger each day.

Moreover, the pollution of our environment caused by the animal food industry causes more damage to our environment and to the climate than all the forms of modern transportation in our world combined.

To live our lives with responsibility and care for our environment, the work of the Creator, is our religious duty; and especially towards sentient beings whom we are instructed to treat with compassion and mercy.

Our sages declared that true children of ABRAHAM OUR FATHER are merciful, modest, and behave with lovingkindness towards others (TALMUD BAVLI, YEVAMOT 99a), and the GEMARA goes even further in suggesting that therefore one who does not behave with compassion is not truly of the seed of ABRAHAM OUR FATHER (TALMUD BAVLI, BEITZAH 32b). Thus all who seek the welfare of their souls and strive to cleave to the attributes of the Holy One Blessed Be He, will avoid consuming any products that are the result of these abovementioned most serious transgressions.

RABBI DAVID ROSEN,
Former Chief Rabbi of Ireland

HASKAMA to "BEFORE THE BLIND"
By ASA KEISAR

IT is a great honor to write a short HASKAMA to the book "BEFORE THE BLIND" by the scholar ASA KEISAR.

This book is a great KIDDUSH HASHEM.

Over the years the topic of the prohibition of TZA'AR BA'ALEI CHAYIM has unfortunately been neglected by many religious Jews. The truth is that this prohibition should be at the center of our attention. The careful treatment of animals has been the hallmark of the Jewish tradition and was one of the greatest foundations of HALACHA. According to many Halachic authorities this prohibition is not even a Rabbinical one but rather a TORAH prohibition – "MIDE'ORAITA", and of the highest urgency.

In many ways it is the touching stone on which Judaism stands as it exemplifies Judaism's sensitivity to the feelings of all of God's creations. Thus, violating this law puts all of Judaism in a bad light, undermining its great teachings and losing its very mission.

One can therefore not be thankful enough to **Chacham Asa Keisar** for writing this book in which he spells out all

7 Cassuto Street, Jerusalem, 9643307, Israel
Tel: +972-2-6427272   Fax: +972-72-2400108
office@cardozoacademy.org ● www.cardozoacademy.org

the biblical and Rabbinical commandments pertaining to looking after the world of animals and protecting them in every way possible.

This is all the more important today, when the huge consumption of animal flesh has become common and tens of thousands of animals are killed or slaughtered daily. Even when the merciful laws of SHECHITA are properly applied, there is much evidence that prior to SHECHITA these animals are mishandled and hurt in a way that Judaism would never agree to.

The question is then whether this meat is still KOSHER although the laws of SHECHITA have been observed.

Any sensitive Jew should therefore carefully study this book, and ask himself or herself whether they live up to the high standards which this book demands from us, and how we truthfully need to deal with the animal world.

May **Chacham Asa Keisar** be blessed by GOD for having written this most important and crucial book.

May it be read and practiced by every proud Jew!

RABBI NATHAN LOPES CARDOZO

7 Cassuto Street, Jerusalem, 9643307, Israel
Tel: +972-2-6427272   Fax: +972-72-2400108
office@cardozoacademy.org ❖ www.cardozoacademy.org

BS"D Heshvan 9, 5779

Congratulatory Letter

I received the wonderful book of Rabbi Asa Keisar "Before the Blind" dealing with the important prohibition on causing suffering to animals (Tza'ar Ba'alei Chayim) which a lot of the food industry is transgressing. This is evident in the way they raise and treat the animals, and in the way they kill them [allowing one animal to witness the killing of another] as well as all the cruelty surrounding these practices.

The author has collected hundreds of articles by sages from all the generations and has methodically analyzed all of the opinions expressed on this prohibition in the halachic and Torah view. I doubt if what the author is suggesting – that the public stop eating meat – will help stop these cruel practices. First, because the people whose spirit is shaken by this prohibition are still a small part of the population, and second, because the industry is making a lot of money out of it, and it will not agree to change the practices used today in raising and killing animals. They make large profits and would not want to diminish them.

Therefore, it would be appropriate for the government to become involved and pass laws that would change the way animals are being raised and killed. The Ministry of Agriculture, with the veterinarians, have the power to change the current situation. Moral and inspired people are few and have little influence, but things can change for the good when the public wakes up and pressures the government.

In any case, **Rabbi Asa Keisar**'s book represents an important awakening call. It also makes a statement towards heaven and a protest by every reader of the book who does not agree nor participate with the transgressions performed today.

Just a little light dispels much darkness in the world.

Rabbi Moshe Zuriel

Author of more than 50 books, including: "OTSROT HARAV KOOK" (seven volumes), "OTSROT HAMUSAR" and more…

B"H MONDAY, ADAR 9, 5781

Congratulatory Letter

I have received the book **"BEFORE THE BLIND"** written by the sage **R. ASA KEISAR** on the subject of the treatment of animals. The book contains an impressive compilation of our Jewish sources, from the Bible to the great sages of recent generations. According to the author in the introduction to this book, he has not come to innovate anything but rather to mention known things as it says in the RAMCHAL's introduction to his foundational book "MESILAT YASHARIM".

Sometimes higher levels hide the foundational ones on which the entire building stands. The book of Genesis contains the foundations of human existence as well as our national existence on many and varied levels. Reading the first chapter of THE TORAH awakens us to realize that animals were not created for the purposes of man but rather for him to be responsible for their existence. The food a person needs is in the plant world. After the flood, when humanity descended from its previous moral level, man's status was equated to that of a carnivorous animal, and he was allowed to shed animal blood, while being forbidden to eat blood and of course to harm his own species. THE TORAH reduced the number of animal species allowed to be eaten, but still calls eating them "hunting" and "blood spilling": **"Every person of the children of Israel, as well**

as of those foreigners living within them, who will hunt an edible animal or bird and kill it, must cover its blood with dirt - וְאִישׁ אִישׁ מִבְּנֵי יִשְׂרָאֵל וּמִן־הַגֵּר הַגָּר בְּתוֹכָם אֲשֶׁר יָצוּד צֵיד "חַיָּה אוֹ־עוֹף אֲשֶׁר יֵאָכֵל וְשָׁפַךְ אֶת־דָּמוֹ וְכִסָּהוּ בֶּעָפָר" (Leviticus 17, 18). Hunting is the occupation of Nimrod and Esau and is not the way of the People of Israel, and 'blood spilling' is certainly an expression relating to the prohibition to murder humans, associated here with an animal or chicken slaughterer. It is clear that THE TORAH expresses reservations regarding the killing of animals, even those it allowed to be eaten. The Prophet ISAIAH twice prophesies that in the future even the lion will be vegetarian and eat hay (ISAIAH 11:7 ; 65:25).

Mankind is advancing towards the rectification of ancient sins. Part of this progress is made by returning to the original plan that humans be nourished from the plants destined for them. The fear that nestles in the hearts of many that the time has not yet come for this is misplaced. Precisely in a world that enjoys an abundance of natural foods at the grace of the Blessed Creator, the possibility of returning to the roots is easy and simple. It will also strengthen morals towards human beings, and save complicated halachic problems regarding the KASHRUT of food.

Again I wish to congratulate the honored author for his blessed initiative to write this book, and wish him and us that this issue become a central one in the nation of Israel and in the whole world.

RABBI BENAYAHU BRUNNER,
President of the Safed Hesder Yeshiva

The Ludwig and Erica Jesselson **Institute for Advanced Torah Studies**
המכון הגבוה לתורה ע״ש לודביג ואריקה יסלזון

B"H, AV 11, 5778 / 23.07.18

A sa Keisar has done a great deed by filling his granary with a collection of our sages' teachings.

These teachings, sweeter than honey, are aimed to piously distance us from any kind of cruelty toward animals ("Tza'ar Ba'alei Chayim").

For his mercies are on all his works and anyone who has compassion for God's creatures will have compassion for human beings and will receive compassion from heaven.

Therefore it is appropriate to learn and absorb the sweetness of this book, "Before the Blind", to study, teach and do, and the Lord will pay his due to his followers.

Rabbi Daniel Sperber

The Midrasha

Bar-Ilan University, Ramat Gan 5290002 אוניברסיטת בר-אילן, רמת גן
Tel. 03-531-8608/270 טל. Fax: 03-738-4025 פקס.
Email: biu.midrasha@gmail.com, Web: www.midrasha.biu.ac.il

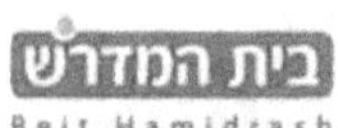
Beit Hamidrash

Bar-Ilan University, Ramat Gan 5290002 אוניברסיטת בר-אילן, רמת גן
Tel. 03-531-8479 טל. Fax: 03-738-4023 פקס.
Email: biu.beit.hamidrash@gmail.com, Web: www.mgl.org.il

I have not come to teach men that which they do not know, but to remind them of what they already know and is very evident to them, for you will find in most of my words only things which most people know, and concerning which they have no doubts.

I have said in my heart (DEVARIM 1:17): **"You shall not tremble before any man, for the judgment is God's -** לֹא תָגוּרוּ מִפְּנֵי־אִישׁ כִּי הַמִּשְׁפָּט "לֵא־לֹהִים הוּא".

And since my intent is only to do the will of my Creator, I have mustered the strength to gird the words of our holy TORAH and our Rabbis, and I have named this work based upon its first topic.

The reader should not be surprised that I have chosen one specific commandment to focus upon, for it is based upon what our TORAH states (DEVARIM 13:18): **"And he will give you mercy and be merciful** -"וְנָתַן־לְךָ רַחֲמִים וְרִחַמְךָ".

"As long as one remains cruel-natured, GOD acts accordingly towards him, for GOD acts mercifully only towards the merciful".
(OHR HACHAYIM - DEVARIM 13:18)

In addition, to shed light unto blind eyes is unto itself a MITZVAH as is warning others of serious transgressions, for THE TORAH states, **"Do not put a stumbling block Before the Blind, and you shall fear your God -** "וְלִפְנֵי עִוֵּר לֹא תִתֵּן מִכְשֹׁל וְיָרֵאתָ מֵאֱ־לֹהֶיךָ" (VAYIKRA 19:14). Our sages have explained that this refers to intellectual blindness.

"And God will not withhold good from those who walk in purity -"וַי־הוָה לֹא יִמְנַע־טוֹב לַהֹלְכִים בְּתָמִים" (PSALMS 84:12).

ASA KEISAR

"ONE
must also have mercy
upon animals, because it is
forbidden to cause undue pain
or anguish to an animal.

Concerning this, THE TORAH says
(DEVARIM 22:4), **'You must surely lift it up
with him** (with his animal's load) - הָקֵם תָּקִים עִמּוֹ׳.

In addition, according to Jewish law, one is
obligated to feed his animals, before he himself
eats. (BERACHOT 40a).

The attribute of mercy is the mark of the CHILDREN
OF ABRAHAM, THE SEED OF ISRAEL, (YEVAMOT 79a), as
THE TORAH states (DEVARIM 13:18): **'And grant you
mercy, and He will be merciful toward
you, and multiply you** - וְנָתַן־לְךָ רַחֲמִים
וְרִחַמְךָ וְהִרְבֶּךָ׳.

(ORCHOT TZADDIKIM,
  THE GATE OF MERCY)

Table Of Contents

"As long as one
remains cruel-natured,
God acts accordingly towards
him, for God acts mercifully
only towards the merciful".
(Ohr HaChayim - Devarim 13:18)

INTRODUCTION

Recently investigations into the cruel practices, used in the production of animal-based food have been made public. This issue has convinced some people to no longer consume animal-based products. However, others claim the information was taken out of context and leads the public astray. The rising tide of interest in this issue has brought about public debate and raised the following question: how does JUDAISM perceive this phenomenon?

Accepted practices in the industry of animal-based food production include, but are not limited to:

- CUTTING OFF THE BEAKS OF CHICKS with no anesthesia;

- GRINDING MALE CHICKS alive in steel grinders;

- KILLING CHICKENS by electrocution;

- SEPARATING CALVES from their mothers immediately after birth;

- CAGING CALVES in narrow stalls to disable even minimal movement;

- INJECTING HORMONES to animals so that they will grow at an abnormal rate and produce an abnormal amount of eggs. This causes the animals to develop various diseases;

- PHYSICAL ABUSE.

The meat, dairy and egg industries, which have existed for only a few decades, commit very grave TORAH transgressions. As a result of this reality, there is an ongoing debate among the public and religious circles regarding the KASHRUT of these products. How can a food product be KOSHER if it is obtained by transgressing the commandment not to cause anguish and pain to an animal?

In the coming chapters, we will deal with this issue.

DO NOT PLACE A STUMBLING BLOCK BEFORE THE BLIND

We shall begin with the halachic ruling rendered by Rabbi Yosef Chayim zt"l written in his book "Ben Ish Chai":

❝ In all cases, when an animal or bird observes another being slaughtered, its lungs will contract due to the fear it experiences. And the established rule states, a lung that is fully or even partially contracted, if caused by humans who frightened the animal, such as by slaughtering another animal before its eyes or the like, this animal is ruled as Treif (I.e., eating it is prohibited). Therefore, in large towns where many people congregate to have their chickens slaughtered, and the Shochet slaughters the birds before them, while they hold live birds in their arms; there is concern this will cause the chicken's lungs to contract as well as cause unnecessary pain to animals. People should therefore stand at a distance from the SHOCHET so the chickens will not see others being slaughtered and be aware of their own fate".

(BEN ISH CHAI, SECOND YEAR, TAZRI'AH, HALACHA 15)

Thus wrote RABBI EPHRAYIM ZALMAN MARGOLIS:

❚❚I have seen people who come to the SHOCHET holding birds while standing near and next to him [...] so they will be next to have their birds slaughtered and this causes pain to animals [...] and there is no greater animal suffering than this! It is obvious that we cannot claim that birds do not feel pain, for it is stated in chapter 36, that at times the lungs contract due to fear of seeing the animal ahead of it being slaughtered".

(RESPONSA BEIT EPHRAIM, YOREH DE'AH, SIMAN 26)

We also see this ruling prohibiting the slaughter of one living creature before another due to causing pain and suffering to animals, by RABBI YECHIEL MICHEL HALEVI EPSTEIN, the author of "ARUCH HASHULCHAN". In his words:

❚❚Thus, it is proper for the SHOCHET to be careful not to slaughter one animal in front of another [...] and there is the issue of causing undue pain to animals; it is absolutely forbidden and some of the Great ACHRONIM have written this as well".

(ARUCH HASHULCHAN, YOREH DE'AH, TREFOT 36, HALACHA 70)

In today's KOSHER slaughter houses the slaughtering process is not carried out in accordance with Jewish Halachic law. The process is carried out in a factory-like "conveyor belt" manner, thus each animal is slaughtered directly in front of the next: This HALACHA prohibiting the slaughtering of one animal in front of another informs us of the severity of the prohibition. Therefore, before we continue, let us point out the source of this TORAH commandment. We will then quote Our Rabbis' words reflecting on this MITZVAH and the degree to which it must be observed. Since animals cannot speak, we will bring the words of our sages specifying precisely what causes an animal anguish. After we learn the prohibition, we will inform the reader what occurs in today's factories producing animal products, proceeding to tie together all of our learning with practical guidelines. ❧❧

MITZVOT PREVENTING
TZA'AR BA'ALEI CHAYIM

‏"שֵׁשֶׁת יָמִים תַּעֲשֶׂה מַעֲשֶׂיךָ וּבַיּוֹם הַשְּׁבִיעִי תִּשְׁבֹּת לְמַעַן יָנוּחַ שׁוֹרְךָ‎
‏וַחֲמֹרֶךָ:"‏ (שְׁמוֹת כ״ג, י״ב)

"You may do your work six days, but on the seventh day you must cease; so that your ox and your donkey may rest".

(SHEMOT 23:12)

‏"וְנָתַתִּי עֵשֶׂב בְּשָׂדְךָ לִבְהֶמְתֶּךָ וְאָכַלְתָּ וְשָׂבָעְתָּ:"‏ (דְּבָרִים י״א, ט״ו)

"And I will provide grass in your field for your animals, and you will eat and be full".

(DEVARIM 11:15)

‏"כִּי יִקָּרֵא קַן־צִפּוֹר | לְפָנֶיךָ בַּדֶּרֶךְ בְּכָל־עֵץ | אוֹ עַל־הָאָרֶץ אֶפְרֹחִים‎
‏אוֹ בֵיצִים וְהָאֵם רֹבֶצֶת עַל־הָאֶפְרֹחִים אוֹ עַל־הַבֵּיצִים לֹא־תִקַּח הָאֵם‎
‏עַל־הַבָּנִים: שַׁלֵּחַ תְּשַׁלַּח אֶת־הָאֵם וְאֶת־הַבָּנִים תִּקַּח־לָךְ לְמַעַן יִיטַב‎
‏לָךְ וְהַאֲרַכְתָּ יָמִים:"‏ (דְּבָרִים כ״ב, ו')

"If you should chance upon a bird's nest before you on the road in any tree, or on the ground, [with] fledglings or eggs, and the mother is sitting on the fledglings or on the eggs; do not take the mother with her offspring. You must surely send away the mother and the offspring take for yourself, so that you will benefit and you will live long".

(Devarim 22:6)

"לֹא־תַחְסֹם שׁוֹר בְּדִישׁוֹ:"

(דְּבָרִים כ״ה, ד׳)

"You may not muzzle an ox while it threshes".

(Devarim 25:4)

"לֹא־תַחֲרֹשׁ בְּשׁוֹר־וּבַחֲמֹר יַחְדָּו:"

(דְּבָרִים כ״ב, י׳)

"You may not plow with an ox and with a donkey together".

(Devarim 22:10)

T HE Torah forbids subjecting an animal to anguish, however the commentaries were at odds regarding the question if the prohibition to cause suffering to an animal is a commandment from THE Torah or not.

According to the opinion that it is from THE Torah, we found six sources from where this is learned:

״כִּי־תִרְאֶה חֲמוֹר שֹׂנַאֲךָ רֹבֵץ תַּחַת מַשָּׂאוֹ וְחָדַלְתָּ מֵעֲזֹב לוֹ עָזֹב תַּעֲזֹב עִמּוֹ:״ (שְׁמוֹת כ״ג, ה׳)

"If you see the donkey of your enemy lying under its burden, and you might not want to help him, [but you should] make every effort to help him". (SHEMOT 23:5)

״לֹא־תַחְסֹם שׁוֹר בְּדִישׁוֹ:״ (דְּבָרִים כ״ה, ד׳)

"You may not muzzle an ox while it threshes".

(DEVARIM 25:4)

״הֲלָכָה לְמֹשֶׁה מִסִּינַי״. (רִיטְבָ״א, בָּבָא מְצִיעָא ל״ב: עַל דַּעַת רַשִׁ״י)

"It is a law given to Moshe at Sinai".

(RITVA, BAVA METZIA 32B, ON RASHI'S OPINION)

״וְרַחֲמָיו עַל־כָּל־מַעֲשָׂיו:״ (תְּהִלִּים קמ״ה, ט׳)

"And His mercy is upon all His works". (PSALMS 145:9)

״עַל־מָה הִכִּיתָ אֶת־אֲתֹנְךָ:״ (בְּמִדְבַּר כב, לב)

"Why did you hit your donkey?". (BAMIDBAR 22:32)

״וְהִשְׁקִיתָ אֶת־הָעֵדָה וְאֶת־בְּעִירָם:״ (בְּמִדְבַּר כ, ח)

"And give drink [to] the community and their livestock". (BAMIDBAR 20:8)

THE PROHIBITION TO CAUSE SUFFERING TO AN ANIMAL IS A TORAH COMMANDMENT

Causing suffering to an animal is a TORAH prohibition, and this is the opiniont of THE ROSH[1], THE RIF[2], THE RAMBAM[3] and the majority of RISHONIM[4] and ACHRONIM[5].

In regard to this decision, it is appropriate to mention the words of THE REMA:

---

1   THE MEIRI and THE ROSH - BAVA METZIA (there), and prove from MASECHET SHABBAT.

2   THE RIF, BAVA METZIA 17:2; NIMUKEI YOSEF (there), KESEF MISHNEH, BA'AL HAMA'OR BESHITAT HARIF, MORDECHAI - BAVA METZIA (there).

3   RAMBAM - Halachot Shabbat 25, 26; MOREH NEVUCHIM 3, 17; Laws of a murderer in the annotation of KESEF MISHNEH.

4   SEFER HACHINUCH 550.

5   THE REMA, CHOSHEN MISHPAT, siman 272, 9; OHR SAME'ACH.

> ❝ In acquiring items required for health / medical or other purposes there is no concern for violating the prohibition of Tza'ar Ba'alei Chayim. Therefore, it is permissible to pluck feathers from a living goose and one does not have to fear they are violating Tza'ar Ba'alei Chayim. Nonetheless, this is not done, because it is cruel".
>
> (Rema, Shulchan Aruch, Even Ha'ezer, 5:14)

On the other hand, **Rabbi Naftali Zvi Yehuda Berlin, the Netziv from Volozhin** has written:

> ❝ Those who pluck feathers from birds, after they are slaughtered but not yet dead, are not acting properly. For even an animal that is about to die, as long as it is alive, is subject to the rule of Tza'ar Ba'alei Chayim. Even an animal that has been slaughtered and is convulsing, is subject to the laws of Tza'ar Ba'alei Chayim".
>
> (Responsa Meshiv Davar, part 5, siman 67)

Does **the Rema**'s use of the term "other purposes" mean "any purpose whatsoever"? Such as grinding chicks to death in metal grinders, or electrocuting chickens to death, etc.? (see chapter "**Do animals experience suffering?**") Are these actions permissible for monetary gain? Certainly not!

Responsa Imrei Shefer, Pri Megadim, Api Zutri, and the head of the holy court Virtzburg, **Rabbi Yitzchak Dov HaLevi Bamberger,** clarify **the Rema**'s intent by stating that ONLY for absolute need, such as a mildly sick person, is causing an animal pain permissible, but not for monetary gain.

RABBI ELIYAHU KLETZKIN :

> ❝ Regarding the prohibition of cruelty to animals, if it is permissible to cause suffering to animals for benefit and financial gain?
>
> We must clarify the words of THE REMA (Even HaEzer, SIMAN 5:14) who wrote in 'ISUR VEHETER HA'AROCH - THE LONG PROHIBITION AND PERMIT' (SIMAN 59) that in acquiring any item required for health/medical or other purposes, there is no concern for violating the prohibition of TZA'AR BA'ALEI CHAYIM. It seems that his intent was to permit this only when there was an urgent need such as for medical purposes and other similar urgencies. However, it is not THE REMA's intent to permit these actions for monetary gain. Since some mistakenly believe this prohibition to be completely cancelled in the face of any human need, I have determined that it is necessary to clarify and prove from THE TALMUD and THE POSKIM that this is not so". (RESPONSA IMREI SHEFER, SIMAN 34)

> ❝ On the contrary, in addition to the other commandments regarding animals, one is obligated to suffer monetary loss in order to feed one's animal, for the purpose of preventing TZA'AR BA'ALEI CHAYIM. It is forbidden to transgress any of these commandments for the sake of monetary gain. Even if we would declare this issue an

unresolved contention (DEORAITA VS. DERABANAN) […], THE CHATAM SOFER has already written in YOREH DE'AH (ANSWER 254) that it is clear that we should be strict {not to cause TZA'AR BA'ALEI CHAYIM} […] and all agree that one cannot be lenient". (RESPONSA IMREI SHEFER, SIMAN 34)

RABBI JOSEPH BEN MEIR TEOMIM:

‖ I was asked: a person who had birds, which are called *Kaphiner*, and the birds walk in the garden, and he is afraid that they will fly outside, is it permissible to put a small bone spike in the wings so that they do not fly, or not? And I replied, by himself he will see to prohibit, that cruelty to animals, where there is no great need, is prohibited". (PRI MEGADIM, ORACH CHAYIM, 468:2)

The Gaon and head of the holy court Virtzburg, **RABBI YITZCHAK DOV HALEVI BAMBERGER,** in his letter to BINYAN TZIYON, writes:

‖ A hearty and lengthy debate has concluded that one cannot permit - based on that which REMA has written - that all items required for medical or other purposes are not subject to the prohibition of TZA'AR BA'ALEI CHAYIM. From this we derive only to permit when there is a medical need, even for a mildly sick person. However, we have not permitted this for monetary gain".

(RESPONSA BINYAN TZIYON, SIMAN 108)

RABBI JOSEPH MESSAS:

❚❚ And **RABBI API ZUTRI** was shocked by those who permitted [causing pain to animals], and thus he writes: 'Even if TZA'AR BA'ALEI CHAYIM was a Rabbinic law, how can one presume it is permitted? For medical purposes we lay it aside, but to fulfill one's personal desire, who has allowed us to subject animals to pain?' (API ZUTRI, EVEN HA'EZER, SIMAN 5:25). Hence, even according to those who believe that the prohibition of causing sorrow to animals is DERABANAN, it is still not permissible.

Furthermore, the opinion of the GEONIM and most of the great arbitrators is that it is a Torah prohibition.

And if in grief as relatively mild as plucking feathers is much disputed, how much more so is it grave to cause animals great grief and pain (as is done on a daily basis in the animal-food industry)". (RESPONSA MAYIM CHAYIM, 2, SIMAN 50)

RABBI AVRAHAM PINASO:

❚❚ Where it is done for the purpose of medicine, it is acceptable to us, but to fulfill our lust, who has allowed us animal cruelty?". (API ZUTRI, EVEN HA'EZER, SIMAN 5:25)

RABBI MOSHE FEINSTEIN ZT"L has written:

❚❚ One may not subject an animal to pain and suffering for this is forbidden even if someone will profit from it [...] we see one is not given free rein to cause pain, even if it is for profit from this action [...] it is forbidden to feed an animal things it does not wish to consume, for this is subjecting it to discomfort and it may then suffer with disease and sickness as a result, for this monetary gain comes by cheating others and is forbidden because the prohibition of Tza'ar Ba'alei Chayim is a Torah law, which forbids one from subjecting an animal to pain and suffering". (Responsa Igrot Moshe, Even Ha'ezer, part 4, section 92)

Thus, **Rabbi Ovadia Yosef ZT"L** has written:

❚❚ Based on what has been stated, we say that the only permission given is when there is a great need such as for immediate medical purposes".

(Responsa Yabia Omer, part 10, Yoreh De'ah, siman 58)

Rabbi Yitzchak HaLevi Hertzog ZT"L writes,

❚❚ A question from the office of the Rabbinate of Israel was posed to me: in the operation of chicken coops in Israel, is it permissible to remove part of the beak of the birds to prevent them from pecking at other birds. The cutting would be performed by skilled laborers so that there would be no blood, and they would cut only the top of the beak, far from the nostrils.

[...] We must always be concerned with Tza'ar Ba'alei Chayim which is a Torah prohibition. It is already decided in Shulchan Aruch (Even Ha'ezer siman 5, section 14, In the Rema) on the basis of rulings from the Rabbi Israel Isserlein, (Siman 105, and 'Isur VeHeter Ha'Aroch - The long prohibition and permit', siman 59, section 36) that regarding all items required for medical or other human needs, there is no concern for Tza'ar Ba'alei Chayim. However, Rabbi Eliyahu Kletzkin in his book "Imrei Shefer" (section 34) proves from the Talmud and the decisors that the Rema's intent was not to permit Tza'ar Ba'alei Chayim for the sake of monetary profit but rather only for a pressing need such as a medical one, or for the benefit of the animal itself".

(Psakim & Ketavim, Yoreh De'ah, siman 7)

In our days, we must also be concerned with the possibility of Chilul Hashem, i.e., desecration of God's name, for Jews are called "merciful ones, the children of merciful ones" and we must be a light unto the nations; and we are witnessing a growing phenomenon taking place in Israel and throughout the entire world, of ethical people rising and protesting against the cruel abuse taking place in the animal food factories.

In the animal-food industry they separate the calf from the mother immediately after it is born, making it impossible for the mother to nurse her newborn. The young offspring cannot nurse from its mother. This is contrary to the spirit of Torah, for our sages have said about King Solomon's verse **"The righteous know the soul of their animal -** יוֹדֵעַ צַדִּיק נֶפֶשׁ בְּהֶמְתּוֹ**"** (Proverbs 12:10), that this is referring to God who has written in His Torah, **"When an ox or a sheep or a goat is born, it shall remain under its mother for seven days -** שׁוֹר אוֹ־כֶשֶׂב אוֹ־עֵז כִּי יִוָּלֵד וְהָיָה שִׁבְעַת יָמִים תַּחַת אִמּוֹ**".**

(Vayikra Rabbah 27:11)

The Malbim (Rabbi Meir Leibush ben Yehiel Michel Wisser) states:

❚❚ The Tzadik is one who acts with righteousness. Not only do they act righteously with human beings but also towards the animals in their possession. They know an animal's nature to give it food at the appropriate times and in the proper amount and not to exceed its capacity to work, for these too are the laws of wisdom and righteousness. As it is written in THE TORAH, 'I will give grass in the fields for your animals - וְנָתַתִּי עֵשֶׂב בְּשָׂדְךָ לִבְהֶמְתֶּךָ' (Devarim 11:15) and afterwards is it written, 'And you will eat and be sated - וְאָכַלְתָּ וְשָׂבָעְתָּ' (there). From this sequence we learn that we must feed our animals before we ourselves eat, and more generally - that the prohibition to subject animals to anguish is a TORAH law.

[...] But the evil person acts not with righteousness but the opposite; even if you see them act mercifully you can be assured their "mercy" emanates from a deeply ingrained cruelty. For instance, they may act "mercifully" towards those they hold captive and would not kill them, thus enabling the captive to serve their needs. With regard to acting mercifully towards animals, an evil person may enlarge his animal's food portions, for instance, merely to increase the animal's heavy workload. These people's "mercy" is rooted in their self-serving nature".

(THE MALBIM ON PROVERBS 12:10)

These positions have been heard from the great sages of Israel throughout the generations.

RASHI [RABBI SHLOMO YITZCHAKI]:

> ❝A righteous person knows the nature of his animal -
> specifically, what his animal needs❞.

RABBI DAVID ALTSCHULER [METZUDAT DAVID]::

> ❝The righteous person pays attention even to the needs
> of his animal to fulfill its craving, because GOD greatly
> values mercy❞.

Now we will bring our sages' words regarding the prohibition of separating a calf from its mother at birth.

RABBI YITZCHAK HEBENSTREIT (Author of the book 'Doresh Hamudot'):

> ❝It is stated in THE TALMUD (PESACHIM 112): 'Greater than
> the calf's desire to suckle is the mother's desire to
> nurse'. Therefore, THE TORAH has commanded, 'When an
> ox or a sheep or a goat is born, it shall remain under
> its mother for seven days - שׁוֹר אוֹ־כֶשֶׂב אוֹ־עֵז כִּי יִוָּלֵד
> וְהָיָה שִׁבְעַת יָמִים תַּחַת אִמּוֹ' (VAYIKRA 22:27). Thus, for the first
> seven days of the baby's life, it is forbidden to separate the
> child from the mother, because doing so during the first
> seven days is the most extreme form of cruelty of which
> there is no greater. And we find in THE TALMUD (TA'ANIT
> 16, and look at the JERUSALEM TALMUD there) that when the people
> of NINEVEH wanted to win GOD's favor, they housed

animals separated from their mothers; for example: calves inside the shed and their mothers outside or colts outside and its mother inside; each one crying out for the other. And the people of NINEVEH cried out loudly to GOD and said, "If You have no mercy upon us, we will have no mercy upon the animals, but if you show mercy to us, we will have mercy upon these animals".

(RABBI YITZCHAK HEBENSTREIT: BOOK KIVROTH HATTA'AVAH)

On the verse (VAYIKRA 22:27): **"When an ox or a sheep or a goat is born, it shall remain under its mother for seven days"** - ‏"שׁוֹר אוֹ־כֶשֶׂב אוֹ־עֵז כִּי יִוָּלֵד וְהָיָה שִׁבְעַת יָמִים תַּחַת אִמּוֹ"‏ - RABBI MENACHEM MENDEL SCHNEERSON, THE LUBAVITCHER REBBE expounds:

❚❚The concept of mercy is understood from childhood, to mean that a human may not subject an animal to anguish or pain [...] And right after this verse THE TORAH states (VAYIKRA 22:32): **'Do not desecrate my holy name -** ‏'וְלֹא תְחַלְּלוּ אֶת־שֵׁם קָדְשִׁי'‏ [...], for this command stems from mercy and is understood to mean that we may not subject a mother animal to pain by separating her from her child immediately after birth".

(TORAT MENACHEM HITVADUYOT 5744/1984, PART 3, PAGE 1665)

RABBI MENASHE KLEIN:

❚❚The rationale of this commandment is that GOD almighty, the Father of mercy is merciful towards all of His creations, even towards animals. Therefore, when He commanded that an animal remain with its mother for seven days it was intended to give pleasure to the mother so she could enjoy the fruit of her womb[6]. For this reason, THE TORAH states (VAYIKRA 22:28): **"An ox or a sheep may not be slaughtered on the same day as its child"** - **"וְשׁוֹר אוֹ־שֶׂה אֹתוֹ וְאֶת־בְּנוֹ לֹא תִשְׁחֲטוּ בְּיוֹם אֶחָד"** - because GOD shows mercy to all of His creations and to slaughter an animal and its child on the same day is a display of cruelty; and it is not fitting for any Jew to act with cruelty at any time. GOD has therefore commanded us establish within our souls the positive attributes of pity and mercy while inhibiting and distancing us from acting cruelly".

(RABBI MENASHE KLEIN, RESPONSA MISHNEH HALACHOT, PART 4, SIMAN 239)

RABBI YITZCHAK ZELLER:

❝ 'It shall remain under its mother for seven days - **וְהָיָה שִׁבְעַת יָמִים תַּחַת אִמּוֹ'** (VAYIKRA 22:27) - The rationale of this commandment is that GOD is the Father of mercy 'and has mercy on all of his creations - **וְרַחֲמָיו עַל־כָּל־מַעֲשָׂיו'** (PSALMS 145:9), even animals. As the verse states, 'It shall remain under its mother for seven days - **וְהָיָה שִׁבְעַת יָמִים תַּחַת אִמּוֹ'**, to give pleasure to its mother".

(YALKUT YITZCHAK, MITZVA 294)

RABBI AVRAHAM SABA:

❝ And not earlier, because that is cruelty".

(TZROR HAMOR, VAYIKRA, EMOR)

---

6   See SEFER MITZVOT HASHEM [by RABBI BARUCH HALPERIN]: MITZVAH 295 [Not to slaughter an animal and its son in one day], and in RABBI JOSEPH BABAD's book: MINCHAT CHINUCH

RABBI AVRAHAM YITZCHAK KOOK:

❚❚Based on the complete and whole view, which is full of **GOD**'s kindness to all of His creations, a person should realize that the purpose of the milk from an animal mother's breast is to nourish her baby and not for people to use as they please. Specifically, it is for nursing the young baby, the beloved kid, from her breast and the kid should take pleasure nursing from its beloved mother's breast".

(RABBI AVRAHAM YITZCHAK KOOK, THE VISION OF VEGETARIANISM AND PEACE)

DO **ANIMALS** EXPERIENCE SUFFERING?

MAIMONIDES states:

> ❙❙ There is no distinction between anguish experienced by a human and anguish experienced by animals; this is because the love and yearning of a mother for its offspring is not dependent upon intelligence but rather on the inherent nature found in most creatures as it is found in man". (MOREH NEVUCHIM [=GUIDE FOR THE PERPLEXED], 3:48)

NACHMANIDES states:

> ❙❙ Animals experience concern and there is no distinction between the concern of a human and the concern of an animal for its children, because the love of a mother towards its offspring from its womb is not dependent

upon intelligence or speech. Rather, it is a function of the consciousness that is found in animals and human beings alike".

(RAMBAN, DEVARIM 22:6)

There is a difference of opinion between **MAIMONIDES** and **NACHMANIDES** specifically regarding the reason of the commandment, not whether or not an animal can experience anguish. **MAIMONIDES'** understanding is that the commandant is straightforward; one may not cause anguish to an animal. **NACHMANIDES** is of the opinion that the purpose of the commandment is to direct us onto the straight path and to uproot cruelty from man.

RABBI SAMSON RAPHAEL HIRSCH states:

> ❚❚ Just as a human feels pain, so too do animals feel and sense if they are cut, pushed, smitten, overworked, in fear and panic, hungry and thirsty. At times, a person may forget this because he is self-absorbed or hoping to complete a plan or by being unaware, or out of a desire to be cruel, and thus might cause anguish to his animal, torturing and causing pain to the soul of a living creature".

(HOREB, 5:1)

RABBI YITZCHAK HEBENSTREIT:

> ❚❚ I will explain the rationale of the Rabbinic statement, **"it is forbidden to place the eggs of a different species of bird into the nest of another species because of TZA'AR BA'ALEI CHAYIM"**. At first glance we do not understand

what anguish the animal experiences; however, scientists have determined that feelings of anguish, sadness, mercy and anger found in humans, are also found in animals".

(Rabbi Yitzchak Hebenstreit: book Kivroth hatta'avah)

Now
that we have LEARNED
that the prohibition
of causing anguish
and suffering
to animals
IS A TORAH LAW,
AND NOW
that we have SEEN
what causes
anguish
to an animal,
we will PRESENT
some
of the transgressions
occurring
in the animal-food manufacturing
ACROSS
THE
GLOBE.

🍂 **GRINDING CHICKS TO DEATH** - in egg manufacturing - in the chicken hatcheries, all male chicks are ground to death, by metal teeth, in a machine, **WHILE THEY ARE ALIVE,** because they have no economic value, since they do not produce eggs. In the manufacturing of chicken meat, they grind all of the chicks that have defects, both male and female. **IN TOTAL, EVERY YEAR 10 MILLION CHICKS ARE GROUND UP ALIVE IN ISRAEL ALONE.**

🍂 **CHOPPING OFF BEAKS OF ALL CHICKENS IN EGG MANUFACTURING WITHOUT ANESTHETIC.** This is done by using a machine with a cutting blade heated to 700 degrees Celsius.

🍂 **CONFINING CALVES REARED FOR VEAL IN VERY SMALL CAGES DISABLING EVEN MINIMAL MOVEMENT,** giving them minimal amounts to eat, for the purpose of making their flesh delicate and soft.

🍂 **GENETIC ALTERATIONS ◊ DENSELY PACKED CAGE PHYSICAL TORTURE ◊** Sheep and cattle shipped from other countries in highly concentrated groups **UNDER BRUTAL CONDITIONS** and additional travesties.

🍂 **ELECTROCUTING HENS TO DEATH** - after hens can no longer withstand the burden of laying eggs, they are electrocuted by passing an electrical current through the water trough in each cage. The birds are scheduled for killing every two years. **IN ISRAEL ALONE MORE THAN 4 MILLION CHICKENS ARE KILLED IN THIS MANNER PER YEAR.**

🍂 In milk production, **ALL CALVES ARE SEPARATED FROM THEIR MOTHERS AT BIRTH.**

🍂 **CUTTING OFF HORNS WITHOUT ANESTHETIC** - all of the milking cows have their horns removed by means of a chemical solution.

🍂 **BIRDS ARE SLAUGHTERED IN ASSEMBLY LINE FASHION,** where they see the others in front of them being slaughtered, as it is with larger animals.

This is the face of an industry focused on maximizing profits while paying no attention to cruelty and thus seriously transgressing TORAH commandments.

Note how strict our Rabbis, of blessed memory, were on this issue of not subjecting animals to suffering and certainly not to extreme anguish.

Thus it is written in the book "PELE YOETZ", BY RABBI ELIEZER PAPO:

> ❚❚ 'The wise man, hearing them, will gain more wisdom - 'יִשְׁמַע חָכָם וְיוֹסֶף לֶקַח' (Proverbs 1:5). RABBI YEHUDA THE CHASSID did not ever raise chickens, as he feared that he would be unable to be careful enough not to cause them anguish […] and stated, it is not advisable for a person to raise birds […] for one is responsible to feed them, and the sin and punishment for not doing so is great".
>
> (PELE YOETZ, SECTION: ANIMALS)

Now, after we have learned about the prohibition and the processes existent in modern manufacturing, we must ask if it is permitted to consume meat, milk products and eggs resulting from TORAH transgressions, i.e., from violating the commandment not to subject animals to anguish?

This is a very demanding and serious question and we must deal with it. Consider that in biblical times there was no mass manufacturing as there is today and there was no anguish caused to animals. When they were milked, they allowed the calf to suckle as well and it was not separated from its mother, thus there was no anguish. They did not cut off chickens' beaks, the chicken coops were not densely packed (today the living space for each hen is 20 centimeters), chicks were not ground up alive, and were never electrocuted. In the past, animals seldom, if ever, experienced anguish caused by people throughout their lives.

For something to be considered Kosher, we know that it is not sufficient just for the item to be of a Kosher substance; the means of producing it also needs to be Kosher. What makes something Kosher is not only the substance of what it is, but how it was produced. For example, a stolen item is forbidden to use even if it can be used for a Mitzvah. Another example would be wine or bread made by a non-Jew. Although the wine and bread may be kosher, nevertheless they are forbidden for consumption. These prohibitions result from how these inherently-Kosher items were produced. According to the laws of Kashrut it is not sufficient for an item to be of Kosher substance; the means by which it has been obtained are no less important.

Therefore, we ask: why is Chametz that was unknowingly in a Jew's possession during Pesach forbidden, while animal products produced by violating the law that one cannot subject animals to anguish or pain permitted? **How do they differ?**

THE PROHIBITION OF **BENEFITING** FROM A TRANSGRESSION

These are items from which THE TORAH or the sages forbid us to derive benefit. When THE TORAH was given, factory manufacturing did not exist, nor did it exist in the times of the SANHEDRIN. As a result, today we do not have prohibitions stopping us from benefiting from factory produced animal products. However, if there were a SANHEDRIN in our days, they would certainly declare these items as being forbidden to benefit from. When the SANHEDRIN made a decree to forbid deriving benefit from a transgression, it was a specific decree to prevent people from transgressing to begin with. However, since today we do not have a SANHEDRIN to make these kinds of declarations, the responsibility falls upon the consumer.

Nonetheless, we find specific cases where scholars were unwilling to derive benefit from animal suffering (as an individual choice, not applying to the public).

What follows is from the HOLY ZOHAR:

> Birds came and made shade above the heads of the TANA'IM as they studied TORAH, but the TANA'IM did not want to use this shade, and **RABBI PINCHAS BEN YAIR** stated that it caused the birds great anguish to create this shade above them, '**and I do not want to benefit from the exertion of animals**', for THE TORAH verse states (PSALMS 145:9): '**He is merciful towards all his creations** - וְרַחֲמָיו עַל־כָּל־מַעֲשָׂיו'".
>
> (ZOHAR, PART 3, BALAK, PAGE 201)

In the above incident the animals' exertion was initiated by them, and came from their own will, so that no human coercion was involved. Still, **RABBI PINCHAS BEN YAIR** did not want to benefit from this effort. Sensitivity to causing anguish and pain to an animal was deeply ingrained in the souls of the great men of Israel throughout all generations.

In association with this let us quote the words of **RABBI SAMSON RAPHAEL HIRSCH**:

> Note! **GOD**'s TORAH is concerned for all and will oblige you, not only when you desist from unnecessarily causing pain and anguish to animals, but even if you happen to see an animal in pain or anguish, even if it was not your fault and you had nothing to do with its pain,

you are obligated to assist and to save the animal, and to your greatest ability ease its pain and suffering".

(Rabbi Samson Raphael Hirsch, Horeb, 5:2)

Despite all of the above, we do not have an explicit prohibition against derive benefit from animal-based products. Therefore, the clear and absolute prohibition is on purchasing animal products because purchasing means directly supporting modern factory animal production, and supports and promotes the continued violation of Tza'ar Ba'alei Chayim.

"DO NOT PLACE A STUMBLING BLOCK **BEFORE THE BLIND**, AND YOU SHALL FEAR YOUR GOD"

Our Rabbis explain this verse as referring not only to actual blindness but also to intellectual blindness. This commandment is composed of two aspects:

1. The prohibition to give another bad advice.
2. The prohibition to cause or to assist others to commit a transgression.

Sefer HaChinuch:

> ❧ The root of the commandment ["Do not place a stumbling block Before the Blind"]: It is known that repairing the world and settling it is achieved by guiding people and providing them with good advice. This commandment applies everywhere and at all times, and applies to men and women, Jews and non-Jews. One who transgresses this by misleading others with advice that is not beneficial to them or assisting them in committing a transgression, has transgressed a negative commandment and this is compared to transgressing a commandant of the king".
>
> (Sefer HaChinuch, commandment 232)

The Talmud (Avodah Zarah, 6b) establishes that the commandment 'Do not place a stumbling block Before the Blind - וְלִפְנֵי עִוֵּר לֹא תִתֵּן מִכְשֹׁל' - is analogous to two people separated by a river. The river analogy considers a situation where a person will not be able to transgress without the help of the person on the other side.

The **Rishonim**[7] have written that even when it is possible for the sinner to commit a transgression without the help of another, it is still forbidden to assist the transgressor, because according to our sages, assisting one to commit a transgression is always forbidden.

---

7   Shabbat 3, Tosafot, Dibbur HaMatchil: Baba;

Chidushei HaRan, Shabbat 2, Dibbur HaMatchil: Bishla'ma;

Chidushei HaRitva, Bava Metzia 5, Dibbur HaMatchil: de'i lo;

Haran about the Rif, Shabbat 1, Dibbur HaMatchil: Umakshu Hacha

MAIMONIDES rules that:

> ❙❙ one who causes the blind to stumble by giving them faulty advice or by enabling them to commit a sin (the sinner is referred to as blind because their passions blind them from seeing the true path) transgresses a negative commandment, for the verse states, '**Do not place a stumbling block Before the Blind** - וְלִפְנֵי עִוֵּר לֹא תִתֵּן מִכְשֹׁל"'.

(RAMBAM, HILCHOT ROTZEACH AND SHMIRAT NEFESH, 12:14)

MAIMONIDES establishes that when one helps or causes another to a sin, by approaching the sinner who is blinded by desire and assisting him in committing the misdeed, both the sinner and the instigator have violated the law '**Do not place a stumbling block Before the Blind** - וְלִפְנֵי עִוֵּר לֹא תִתֵּן מִכְשֹׁל', as each one assisted the other to commit the sin, whether or not the instigator legitimizes the actual sinful action:

> ❙❙ If he assists in anyway, even by mere speech, he is punished by heaven to the degree of his involvement. However, he is not liable for any punishment mentioned in THE TORAH, but he has violated GOD's word, '**Do not place a stumbling block Before the Blind** - וְלִפְנֵי עִוֵּר לֹא תִתֵּן מִכְשֹׁל' if he caused the sin; additionally, if he helped the sinner to complete the act, they have violated GOD's word (SHEMOT 23:1): '**Do not place your hands with the evil** - אַל־תָּשֶׁת יָדְךָ עִם־רָשָׁע"'.

(MAIMONIDES, COMMENTARY ON THE MISHNA, TERUMOT, CHAPTER 6)

From **MAIMONIDES** we see that assisting a sinner is forbidden by Jewish law not only when they're actively participating in the sinful action – for if one commits a sin in participation with others, it is clear that he has performed a forbidden action. The prohibition applies even when the instigator does not perform an action but rather only causes the sin by helping and encouraging the sinner to commit the infraction. In this situation the sinner is analogous to the blind person with regard to the sin, as he is "blinded" by desire and the instigator misleads him by enabling the sinful action.

In another places **MAIMONIDES** writes:

> ❚❚This prohibition **also includes one who assists** in committing a sin or causes it. The instigator bears responsibility for the sin because he approached an individual whose desire blinded him from seeing and helped to mislead him. Or, the instigator urges the 'blind' with faulty rationale; this is similar to one who lends money and takes interest; both lender and borrower are thus liable for violating the commandment '**Do not place a stumbling block Before the Blind** - וְלִפְנֵי עִוֵּר לֹא תִתֵּן מִכְשֹׁל' since each one helps and enables the other to complete the act. There are numerous similar situations where we say that the two actors assisted each other in committing a sin, and they are both liable for **placing a stumbling block Before the Blind**". (MAIMONIDES, SEFER HAMITZVOT 299)

> ❚❚It is prohibited to purchase a stolen item from a thief, and it is forbidden to support him in altering the item

so that he can sell it; for all who do things of this nature are strengthening the hand of sinners and transgressing the edict Lifnei Iver - Before the Blind".

(Maimonides, Hilchot Gzela and Ave'da, chapter 5)

❚❚ God says, 'Do not place a stumbling block Before the Blind - 'וְלִפְנֵי עִוֵּר לֹא תִתֵּן מִכְשֹׁל', the intent is to one whose vision is obscured by their passion and faulty ideas; one may not increase their blindness or their wayward path. Therefore, **it is forbidden to assist sinners in committing misdeeds, and one may not set a path for another to commit a sin**, rather, we must do the opposite".

(Maimonides, Commentary on the Mishna, Shevi'it, chapter 5:6)

All agree with regard to the concept of "**Two who stand on opposite sides of a river**" that the prohibition is from the Torah. The difference of opinion among the Rishonim is regarding the question: is assisting another to commit a transgression of the law '**Do not place a stumbling block Before the Blind - 'וְלִפְנֵי עִוֵּר לֹא תִתֵּן מִכְשֹׁל** - a Torah law or a Rabbinic law? According to Maimonides, it is a Torah law.

In the Responsa book 'Ktav Sofer' he clarifies that the prohibition to violate Lifnei Iver, that is linked to two, who stand on opposite sides of a river, applies only when the sinner commits the sin with minimal effort. However, it does not apply if the sinner must make a great effort, even if he can commit the act alone, but a conscientious person should be stringent. (Yoreh De'ah, siman 83)

THE REMA explains and is stringent with regard to this prohibition even when the sinner can commit the sin without help.

❚❚ There are those who say that the prohibition to sell them things for idol worship is specifically when there are no others to sell them etc. or that they cannot buy the implements anywhere else. But if they can buy them elsewhere, it is permitted to sell them everything. Some are lenient like the first opinion; however, all people of conscience should be stringent". (THE REMA, YOREH DE'AH, 151:1)

❚❚ And it is forbidden to feed someone who has not washed their hands, as this would be transgressing 'Do not place a stumbling block Before the Blind - וְלִפְנֵי עִוֵּר לֹא תִתֵּן מִכְשֹׁל'". (THE REMA, ORACH CHAYIM, 163:2)

It is pointed out in 'MAGEN AVRAHAM' (163:2) that even when another has access to that food, it is possible that there is a prohibition to assist them in it.

The words of the Ritva (BAVA METZIA 5B) imply that the prohibition to aid another to sin applies **even before the actual offense** and not necessarily at the actual time of the offense.

And this is so also according to the Gra's commentary: (HaGra, Yoreh De'ah, 158:8)

❚❚ And also THE NETZIV FROM VOLOZHIN (IN HIS BOOK MESHIV DAVAR, SIMAN 31) was asked about this, and wrote on behalf of the Rabbi who asked, that there is a difference between assisting another to commit a sin at the time of committing it, and assisting another prior to committing the sin, and wrote that this difference is clear in the opinion of THE TOSAFOT and THE ROSH, noting that also THE BINYAN TZION RESPONSA wrote that, though he added that it is not agreed; and Rashi's opinion is to prohibit the assistance even if it is not at the actual time when the offense is committed [...] and he wrote that the Rambam's opinion is the same as that of Rashi, that even before the sin is committed, it is prohibited to assist in it". (RESPONSA MAYIM CHAYIM, PART 2, SIMAN 51)

And interestingly in the same matter, by RABBI MENASHE KLEIN:

❚❚ Here I have already written in reply to this (LOOK AT SIMAN 123) and I join the warning and the ruling given by the court of RABBI KARELITZ in BNEI BRAK, and signed by the Judges and joined by the MOHARASH VOZNER, AV BEIT DIN ZICHRON MEIR, and the Genius MOHARISH ELYASHIV in the holy city of Jerusalem, joined also by RABBI OVADIA YOSEF, head of the Sefardi decisors, about the evil deed of copying computer discs that contain various softwares and selling them at a low price. And by so doing they are trespassing the boundaries of those who have spent many years and resources in creating these programs, and doing so is an act of delinquency and whoever buys from these offenders is assisting in committing a sin". (RESPONSA MISHNEH HALACHOT, PART 17, SIMAN 122)

And here the question arises, will the purchase be allowed if the sinners are Jews who are apostates and violate the HOLY SHABBAT?

In the Responsa book CHELKAT YA'AKOV (YOREH DE'AH, SIMAN 58) it is asked: **if one is scheduled to work on SHABBAT, can he switch with a non-observant Jew who will work instead and the money earned will go to the person who worked?** Moreover, one who is antagonistic towards Judaism cannot be one's messenger.

The answer is unequivocal and clear: one is not permitted to transgress LIFNEI IVER and it is strictly forbidden because the other Jew is also forbidden to work on SHABBAT, and these are his words:

> ❚❚ it is clear that he is forbidden to work on SHABBAT; as a result it is forbidden for him to command the non-observant to work in his place, as this is like 'two people on either side of the river'. For if he does not order the non-observant Jew to work for him on SHABBAT it is possible that the non-observant Jew would not do any work on SHABBAT even though he does not observe it intentionally; it is possible that he will want to relax this SHABBAT, which is not the case if he replaces the SHABBAT observant Jew since he'll work the entire day: this is literally a case of 'two people on both sides of the river'. If however this was the case of only one person standing at the riverbank and the prohibition would only be that of assisting, we could consider permitting this based on the words of THE SHACH in YOREH DE'AH (chapter 151, section 30) which states that with regard to an apostate,

the prohibition to assist in committing a sin does not apply. My response there on this matter was lengthy. But regarding our case, it is a clear application of two standing on both sides of the river; there is a prohibition of LIFNEI IVER, and this applies even to an apostate or a non-Jew[8]".

(RESPONSA CHELKAT YA'AKOV, YOREH DE'AH, SIMAN 58)

When we make the analogy of one subject to the other, it is clear that it is forbidden (purchasing industrial animal products) for if we do not purchase these products, the fact is that they will not produce them. And even if others do purchase when we do not, the industry's violations will be lessened; it is literally a case of two people on either side of the river.

You may claim we do not buy these products directly from the factory but from the store who bought them from the factory.

This has been discussed by 'PITCHEI TESHUVA' in CHOSHEN MISHPAT (Chapter 356:1):

> ❝ The claim that they did not buy the item directly from the thief but from a Jew is not valid, since they knew they were purchasing an item that was forbidden and they should not have bought it from the first Jew for 'the mouse is not the thief, the hole is!' (KIDDUSHIN 56b). Even though he did not buy directly from the thief, theft is forbidden. And since we are dealing here with theft,

---

8   see PESACHIM 22B, "MINAYIN SHELO YOSHIT" [= From where is it derived that a person may not offer]

there is an additional prohibition on buying from the first buyer who transgressed by buying from the thief; in this case the first buyer is compared to 'the mouse' and the second buyer to 'the hole'".

In regard to the topic of not subjecting animals to pain or anguish we have before us a case analogous to that of 'two people on both sides of the river'; since if not for the purchasing of animal-based products, those who monetarily benefit would not transgress all of THE TORAH prohibitions we have mentioned (see pages 45-46) because they transgress these TORAH prohibitions only to provide us with the products. It is just like something that is stolen and then sold, and certainly the purchasing of it enables the thief to continue to steal again and again, one is dependent upon the other.

The production methods in animal factories are well-known to us today and all of the violations we have mentioned are not incidental; rather, they are the primary methods employed by this industry. Moreover, we are not referring to a situation where a forbidden action is performed for its own purpose, but to a situation where these prohibited actions are being done for us, thus it is literally a case of two people standing on both sides of the river.

One who keeps THE TORAH and the commandments cannot take part in the transgression of TORAH prohibitions and strengthening the hands of those who commit violations by giving them money. It is the purchasing of these goods that enables the continuation of these TORAH infractions. ❧

" It happened in our generation, that the great Kabbalistic Rabbi, Rav Yitzchak Ashkenazi, HaAri, looked in the face of a great scholar and said to him, 'The sin of Tza'ar Ba'alei Chayim is clearly marked on your face!'

The Scholar had great anguish and reflected upon this, until he found that his wife was not giving food to the chickens in the morning. instead she was placing them outside of the gate and into the street to peck. He instructed her to give them wheat bran and water each morning.

After this correction was made, of which Rav Yitzchak was unaware, he looked into the face of the scholar and said to him, 'your sin has dissipated'. He then told Rav Yitzchak what transpired.

From this story it appears that this is following the commandment to **'Walk in His ways - וְהָלַכְתָּ בִּדְרָכָיו'** (Devarim 28:9). i.e. 'Just as He is merciful, so should you be merciful' and it says (Psalms 145:9), **'He has compassion upon all His creations - וְרַחֲמָיו עַל־כָּל־מַעֲשָׂיו".**

(Rabbi Elazar ben Moshe Azikri, Sefer Haredim, Mitzvot As'e, chapter 4)

JOY IS ONLY ATTAINED WITH MEAT AND WINE?

IN the coming chapter we will examine our sages' words with regard to the subject of the joy of eating meat. We will begin with the familiar adage, despite it being mistakenly understood, which is: **"Joy is only attainable with meat and wine"**. We will now quote the entire source of this saying and bring its entire context from THE TALMUD where the sages determine what brings joy to a person on the holidays.

❚❚ Our Rabbis have taught: a man is obligated to bring joy to his children and his entire family on the holiday, as it is written (Devarim 16:14), **'You will be joyous on your holiday - וְשָׂמַחְתָּ בְּחַגֶּךָ'**. What brings joy to a person? Wine! **RABBI YEHUDA** states: men are made joyous by what is suitable to them and women with what is suitable to them. What is suitable for a man? Wine! And for women? Rabbi **YOSEF** says that in Babylonia women found joy in colored garments, while in the land of Israel women found joy in pressed flax garments.

RABBI YEHUDA BEN BETEIRA says: when THE TEMPLE stood, joy was achieved only through eating meat, for the verse states (Devarim 27:7), **'you shall sacrifice peace offerings and eat there and you will be joyous before** Hashem your God - וְזָבַחְתָּ שְׁלָמִים וְאָכַלְתָּ שָּׁם וְשָׂמַחְתָּ לִפְנֵי יְ־הֹוָה אֱ־לֹהֶיךְ'. **However, now that** THE TEMPLE **does not stand, joy is achieved only through wine,** for the verse states (Psalms 104:16), 'Wine will make man's heart happy - וְיַיִן | יְשַׂמַּח לְבַב־אֱנוֹשׁ"'. (TALMUD BAVLI, PESACHIM 109A)

The joy from eating meat, which was brought in the name of **RABBI YEHUDA BEN BETEIRA**, refers only to sacrificial meat, not to 'lust meat' i.e. meat eaten to fulfill a craving, and when THE TEMPLE does not stand, joy is attained only through wine.

RABBI YOSEF KARO:

> ❝ That BARAITA states that in our times only wine brings joy, from which we derive that wine alone is sufficient".
> (BEIT YOSEF, ORACH CHAYIM, SIMAN 529)

RABBI YEHUDAH AYASH:

> ❝ And from this we infer that when THE TEMPLE does not stand, joy is attained only through wine".
> (LECHEM YEHUDAH, HILCHOT CHAGIGA, CHAPTER 1)

I have also seen in the PASSOVER HAGGADAH that the great scholar RABBI YITZCHAK ALACHDAB, son of RABBI SHLOMO ALACHDAB wrote:

> ❚❚ It is clear that in our times, joy on the holiday is attained with wine".

RAMBAM in the LAWS OF YOM TOV (Chapter 6, Halacha 18):

> ❚❚ Men eat meat and drink wine for joy is only achieved with meat and joy is only achieved with wine".

THE BEIT YOSEF declares[9] there is no obligation to eat meat in our days to fulfill the commandment of being joyous on the holiday, for it is stated in THE TALMUD that it is sufficient to drink wine alone and meat is not needed.

The Gaon, RABBI YOSEF DOV SOLOVEITCHIK declares[10] according to MAIMONIDES, that one cannot say that the MITZVAH to be joyful on the holidays in our times is dependent upon eating meat and drinking wine. Rather, it is achieved in the heart through whatever makes a person happy, and it appears from RAMBAM[11] that we can fulfill the commandment to be joyous in a variety of ways.

> ❚❚ GOD commanded us to be joyous on the holidays as it says, 'you shall rejoice on your holidays - וְשָׂמַחְתָּ בְּחַגֶּךָ'

---

9 ORACH CHAYIM, SIMAN 529

10 SHIURIM LEZECHER ABBA MORI ZT"L, PART 2, PAGE 188

11 SEFER HAMITZVOT, MITZVOT ASEH 54; HILCHOT LULAV

[…] What is most required is specifically the drinking of wine, since wine is unique in bringing about joy, and THE TALMUD in PESACHIM says: 'A man is obligated to bring joy to his children and his entire family on the holiday'. What brings joy to a person? Wine'. and it states there, RABBI YEHUDA BEN BETEIRA says: when THE TEMPLE stood, joy was achieved only through eating meat, for the verse states, **'you shall sacrifice peace offerings, eat there and you will be joyous - וְזָבַחְתָּ שְׁלָמִים וְאָכַלְתָּ שָּׁם וְשָׂמַחְתָּ'**. However, now that THE TEMPLE does not stand, joy is achieved only through wine, for the verse states, **'wine will make man's heart happy - וְיַיִן | יְשַׂמַּח לְבַב־אֱנוֹשׁ'** (PSALMS, 104:15)". (MAIMONIDES, SEFER HAMITZVOT, MITZVOT ASEH 54)

MAIMONIDES' intent is to say that at times joy is achieved through wine and at other times (when THE TEMPLE stood) it was achieved with meat, as RAV ELFANDRI, who wrote MIRKEVET HAMISHNEH says:

❝ With regard to the adage "there is no joy other than with meat and there is no joy other than with wine" – the intent of 'there is no joy other than with meat' refers to the joy written about in THE TORAH which is the joy achieved when consuming the meat of the peace offering, as it is written, **'you will sacrifice the peace offering and eat there and be joyous - וְזָבַחְתָּ שְׁלָמִים וְאָכַלְתָּ שָׁם וְשָׂמַחְתָּ'** (DEVARIM 27:7). However, wine also makes one joyous and in our time joy is achieved only through wine; but meat can also make one joyous. However, the primary means through which we achieve joy is wine. Therefore, he wrote: 'men eat meat and drink wine', meaning that there is a time when joy can only be achieved through eating meat and that is when THE TEMPLE stood, when they ate the flesh of the peace offering. But at this time, joy is achieved through wine". (HILCHOT YOM TOV, CHAPTER 6, HALACHA 18)

It is written by **RABBI MENASHE KLEIN** in the RESPONSA MISHNEH HALACHOT:

> ❙❙RAV YEHUDA BEN BAVA states, when THE TEMPLE stood, there was no joy other than with meat, but now that THE TEMPLE does not stand, there is no joy other than with wine. This does not mean that meat does not bring joy; rather, there is no requirement to eat meat since there is no peace offering. But certainly, if one eats meat there is joy and one can fulfill the commandment with meat and wine. But the obligation is to drink wine and from the words of THE TALMUD here there seems to be proof to the Magen Avraham in the laws of Purim where he writes that in our time there is no obligation to eat meat at all". (RESPONSA MISHNEH HALACHOT, PART 7, SIMAN 78)

And I looked in RESPONSA HARASHBASH (BY RABBI SOLOMON BEN SIMON DURAN) (SIMAN 176b) on the question that was asked regarding this issue:

> ❙❙QUESTION: Reuben wants to move from his apartment to another city, so to make himself more expedient he makes an oath not to buy meat, even

on the eve of SHABBAT and holidays; he will not buy meat until he moves. But his move is delayed or things have not worked out as he planned, and he ultimately does not move and regrets his oath. Does he have permission to undue his oath since he only swore that he will not buy meat; perhaps his children can buy meat and he will eat it. Does he have permission or not? What is the ruling with regard to his regret and to the meat he has eaten until this time?

"ANSWER: This oath has validity, since even if he swore specifically not to eat meat on SHABBAT and holidays this does not annul the commandant to be joyous, for the adage, 'there is no joy other than with meat', refers to the meat of offerings eaten in THE TEMPLE. Therefore, they say in THE TALMUD tractate PESACHim in the chapter entitled 'the eve of Passover' that 'when THE TEMPLE stands, there is no joy other than with meat'. Even in the time of THE TEMPLE, if one swears not to eat meat on the holidays, their oath is valid and it does not annul any commandant, because the joy of the holiday is not specifically dependent upon meat, because if the first day of YOM TOV comes out on SHABBAT, they were unable to experience the joy of meat of the CHAGIGAH sacrifice".

And the Gaon and Head of the court RABBI SHLOMO HACOHEN FROM VILNA has written:

❚❚ The primary reason is that consuming the meat of the peace offering is consumption which fulfills a MITZVAH and is a holy act, and doing it brought great joy to body and soul. However, when consuming regular meat which is not associated with any MITZVAH, there is no joy; but wine gives joy to the soul as well".

(RESPONSA BINYAN SHLOMO, HILCHOT SUKKAH, SIMAN 47)

RABBI CHAYIM DAVID HALEVI states:

❚❚ From here, all that was said with regard to the MITZVAH to eat meat, for instance on SHABBAT and YOM TOV, clearly refers to those who eat meat and do not know or are not concerned that it is not healthful. However, those vegans who recognize that eating meat is not healthful, it is clear that they are exempt from enjoying SHABBAT by eating meat, and they should have pleasure with things pleasing and healthful to a wise person".

(RESPONSA ASEH LECHA RAV, PART 5, SIMAN 47)

In the SHULCHAN ARUCH (the Jewish code of law) OUR RABBI YOSEF KARO states that, on SHABBAT:

❚❚ one should increase consumption of meat, wine and sweet delicacies according to their ability".   (SIMAN 250)

The intent of the halachic decisors is not always in the literal meaning of their words, but rather from what is inferred. Thus, one can explain the above law in the following manner: since a person already eats meat during the week, to show respect for SHABBAT they will "increase" their intake to honor the SHABBAT and distinguish it from the week days.

Not all decisors' words are a MITZVAH or a halachic obligation, but rather are merely customs and are not decreed upon the public unless most of the community can fulfill it. Clearly, most of the public consumes meat, so to honor the SHABBAT they should distinguish it from weekdays and for this reason RAV KARO employs the term "increase".

Later on, around 20 years after this law was written in the code of law, RABBI YOSEF KARO writes in his book "MAGGID MEISHARIM" how he was chastised by an angel who had appeared to him:

> ❚❚ You went yesterday to find meat, and you were unsuccessful and lost half a day and even the chickens you found were not suitable. This was my doing, and it was to inform you that meat and wine pull you towards the evil inclination and you should not run after them because a man can live without them. You can honor the SHABBAT without meat, therefore you should cease concerning yourself with anything but GOD's TORAH all day". (MAGGID MEISHARIM, PARASHAT EMOR, FRIDAY, NISSAN 24)

Furthermore, it is written there:

> ❚❚ This is the secret reason why consuming animals' flesh is a base desire, because until Israel had the peace offering they did not eat meat, as is written in the Zohar: MOSES was distressed when Israel requested meat, **and if**

MOSES, peace be upon him, would have entered into the land of Israel with them (the people of Israel), they would not have eaten meat". (MAGGID MEISHARIM, PARASHAT EKEV)

RABBI YEHUDA LEIB CLEARS:

❝ From these words we learn that our Rabbi honored the SHABBAT without eating meat. We see that consuming meat on SHABBAT is not an obligation and even though he wrote in the code of law, chapter 200 subsection 2: 'One should increase consumption of meat, wine and sweet delicacies according to their ability', we have learned that this is not an obligation. The words of the angel are discussed in RESPONSA LEV CHAYIM [BY RABBI HAIM PALACHI] part 2, mark 190". (THE MATTERS OF HALACHA IN THE BOOK OF MAGID MEISHARIM II, 17, SIMAN 250)

RABBEINU YONAH writes that the TANNA did not state that one is "obligated to eat meat", because eating meat and wine on SHABBAT is not an obligation, it is optional (BERACHOT 18A).

RABBI MENASHE KLEIN says In RESPONSA MISHNEH HALACHOT:

❝ Again I have seen in THE SHACH, YOREH DE'AH (chapter 341 section 167) that if one intends to fulfill a MITZVAH, if they wish to eat meat, they may; and if not, they do not have to, for it is not an obligation to eat meat or to drink wine on SHABBAT for they have said, **'Make your Shabbat like a weekday (if you must for shortage of food or money) and do not beg for means from others';**

therefore, one must do all things required on Shabbat, but it is optional whether one chooses to eat meat or not. From this we see there is no Mitzvah at all to eat meat on Shabbat. This is also the opinion of the Magen Avraham who distinguishes between a commandment and an obligation. And certainly, even according to the Shach who has explained the rationale: if one wishes to eat meat since they are intending to do a Mitzvah and they are mindful as they eat to perform a Mitzvah, they fulfill the Mitzvah, but there is no obligation! If so, we can also say this is the opinion of the Magen Avraham. Now we can silence any question about how the halachic decisors, the Achronim and the Magen Avraham hold on the 'obligation' to eat meat".

(Responsa Mishneh Halachot, part 3, siman 31)

Rabbi Chayim Chizkiyahu Medini:

❙❙ Regarding eating meat in our days, our teacher Rav Chayim Benvenisti in the Kneset HaGdolah, Yoreh De'ah, (Siman 28) in the name of Rabbi Solomon Luria states: In our times we rely upon Rabbi Yochanan and Rav Nissim, and one should eat with the intent to strengthen their body [...]

And the Chida in his book 'Chayim Sha'al' (chapter 43, letter 6), writes:

'It is all according to the person, if they can practice self-denial to atone for their sins [...] And we, what will we answer for our orphaned generation with too many sins to count? We are too weak to suffer, the good GOD should atone for us',

Thus he wrote […] for a number of years he abstained entirely from eating meat, and heaven forbid, do not disparage him for happy is his portion [...]

And we have already written in the name of **THE ARI**: 'happy is one who can abstain the entire week from meat and wine' [...]

And on SHABBAT they recline and eat meat and drink wine though this is optional and not an obligation, for it says: 'make your SHABBAT a weekday [if you must – i.e., if you haven't enough money to buy what you need for the meals, and your only choice is to beg]' [...]

And in RESHIT CHOCHMAH (page 117b) he writes at length not to eat any living creature.

We see that one who conducts themselves with discipline and abstains from meat is praiseworthy. See in KEREM SHLOMO, (YOREH DE'AH, SIMAN 1) where he writes at length, that **it is not an obligation to consume meat and wine, even on SHABBAT and holidays.**

In the book 'SHIUR KOMAH' (by RABBI MOSHE KORDOVERO) […] with regard to reincarnation in a KOSHER animal, one who is spiritually wholesome will distance themselves from eating animals, for an evil soul might attach itself to their soul and lead to their downfall and even death […] therefore, **one should not eat meat** unless they have the spiritual insight revealed to them, that the animal from which they eat does not contain the soul of a sinner; this is the warning of **THE ARI**".

(SEDE CHEMED, 1ST PART, ASEFAT DINIM, MA'ARECHET ACHILA)

THE HOLY ALSHEICH [RABBI MOSHE ALSHEICH]:

❚❚You consider yourself just and believe you give fulfillment to animals (by eating them) but you are mistaken [...] Perhaps you will say what greater fulfillment can I give to an animal other than eating it and **raising it to the level of a human, but it is not so**. Because you eat not only the flesh, 'but the blood is its soul'. Thus, on the contrary, I command you to be strong and not to eat the blood; you should be conscious and disciplined not to eat until the soul leaves the animal etc. for the blood is the soul".

(ALSHEICH - DEVARIM 12)

RABBI CHAYIM VITAL:

❚❚I have been severely warned not to slaughter or kill any living thing, not even lice and fleas. My master never killed lice and fleas or any other bug".

(SHA'AR HAGILGULIM, INTRODUCTION 38)

RABBI YITZCHAK HEBENSTREIT:

❚❚One should know that with regard to eating meat, there is an opinion that by consuming meat the animal is raised to the level of speaking man and by this the animal's soul is repaired [...]

There are opposing views on this, and some suggest that on the contrary, one may be guilty of spilling the blood of an animal, and there is no distinction between a scholar and a simpleton since the prohibition to consume meat applies to all. Therefore, one who is spiritually wholesome should not hold the first opinion and claim to be a scholar, but should go in accordance with the stricter, second and more straightforward opinion and not enter into the question of spilling blood, because spilling blood is not a minor issue.

And even if one chooses to go by the first opinion that eating the flesh of an animal repairs its soul, thus only a simpleton would be forbidden to eat meat but not so a Torah scholar. One should not take this as permission to eat meat, and should certainly not consider it a Mitzvah or a benefit or a kindness to the animal. Woe to those who believe this. People should not consider themselves Torah Scholars with regard to eating meat; rather, they should consider themselves simpletons, and even if they are Torah Scholars, they should not consider themselves wiser than their predecessors who ate meat. As **Rav Zera** states (Shabbat 112): **"If the earlier sages were like angels, we are like humans, and if they were like humans we are like donkeys"**. And if they considered themselves Torah Scholars, what can we say? It is not enough for us to be like grasshoppers in our eyes relative to those giants. We must also remember what the giants say about us, 'There are men in the vineyards that are like ants'. And as our scholars said (Berachot 47), **"Who is a simpleton? Some say that even if a person read and learned but did not service**

Torah Scholars, he is a simpleton". So we see, even if one learned and studied but did not service Torah Scholars he is a simpleton. Even if they learned Safra and Sifri and the entire Talmud, they are still considered simpletons because they did not service Torah Scholars and did not learn with them the secrets of the Torah and the Talmud. Furthermore, in tractate Sotah 49 it says: "From the day the Second Temple was destroyed, the generations have deteriorated: scholars have begun to become like scribes that teach children, and scribes have become like ignoramuses". If the original Torah Scholars became like ignoramuses after the destruction, then what can we say about ourselves? Thus, one should not consider themselves a Torah Scholar but an ignoramus, and such are forbidden to eat meat.

I will take this a step further and state that in any case one can never accept the first opinion, that by eating meat one repairs the soul of the animal. This can be proven from an explicit Gemara (Bava Metzia 85): "There was a certain calf that was being led to slaughter. The calf went and hung its head on the corner of Rabbi Yehuda HaNasi's garment and was weeping. Rabbi Yehuda HaNasi said to it: 'Go, as you were created for this purpose'. Then it was said in Heaven: Since he was not compassionate toward the calf, let afflictions come upon him". If you wish to hold according to the first opinion that an animal's soul is repaired by slaughtering and eating it, why then was Rabbi Yehuda punished with afflictions? Didn't he do what was correct by not showing mercy on the calf and telling it go because 'this is why you were created', as in accordance with the first opinion? Moreover, wasn't he doing the calf a favor by urging it to go to slaughter because being slaughtered, it would attain a higher spiritual level? Why was he punished for doing the calf a favor? Does one get punished for doing a MITZVAH? We must conclude from this that RABBI YEHUDA HANASI did not act properly by urging the calf to go to slaughter and indeed it was not created for that purpose; for in general, animals were not created to be slaughtered but for plowing. RABBI YEHUDA HANASI held by this opinion, that an animal is improved by being digested by a human, albeit an ignoramus is forbidden from eating meat for they are no better than animals, but a TORAH Scholar is permitted. However, by afflicting him, Heaven informed RABBI YEHUDA that this is not so. RABBI YEHUDA HANASI was not healed until he reversed his opinion as is related in that GEMARA, and through his retraction his afflictions left him: "**One day, the maidservant of RABBI YEHUDA HANASI was sweeping his house. There were young weasels lying about, and she was in the process of sweeping them out. RABBI YEHUDA HANASI said to her: Let them be, as it is written: 'The Lord is good to all; and His mercies are over all His creations -** טוֹב־יְ־הֹוָה לַכֹּל וְרַחֲמָיו עַל־כָּל־מַעֲשָׂיו:' **(Psalms 145:9). Then they said in Heaven: Since he was compassionate, we shall be compassionate with** him", and he was relieved of his suffering, as it is a major rule (SHABBAT 151) that "Those who have mercy on others, Heaven acts mercifully towards them; and all who do not act mercifully towards others, Heaven does not act mercifully towards them, because it is measure for measure".

I will pose my personal explanation to refute the first opinion that says that an animal's soul benefits by being consumed by a human. If this were so, why are there creatures that are forbidden to be eaten such as impure animals and bugs? Do they not require being repaired like the pure animals with split hooves who chew their cud? Why are these animals excluded? And KOSHER animals, if they are ritually unfit or found to have an imperfection at the time of slaughter, since their consumption is forbidden, how will their souls be repaired? This indicates that the first opinion is not definitive. Thus, one who is spiritually aware will distance themselves from eating animals and follow the stringent opinion. (RABBI YITZCHAK HEBENSTREIT: BOOK KIVROTH HATTA'AVAH)

THE TORAH'S ATTITUDE
TOWARDS EATING MEAT

From THE BOOK OF BERESHIT we learn that at the beginning man was forbidden to eat animals' flesh:

וַיֹּאמֶר אֱ־לֹהִים הִנֵּה נָתַתִּי לָכֶם אֶת־כָּל־עֵשֶׂב ׀ זֹרֵעַ זֶרַע אֲשֶׁר עַל־פְּנֵי כָל־הָאָרֶץ וְאֶת־כָּל־הָעֵץ אֲשֶׁר־בּוֹ פְרִי־עֵץ זֹרֵעַ זָרַע לָכֶם יִהְיֶה לְאָכְלָה: וּלְכָל־חַיַּת הָאָרֶץ וּלְכָל־עוֹף הַשָּׁמַיִם וּלְכֹל ׀ רוֹמֵשׂ עַל־הָאָרֶץ אֲשֶׁר־בּוֹ נֶפֶשׁ חַיָּה אֶת־כָּל־יֶרֶק עֵשֶׂב לְאָכְלָה וַיְהִי־כֵן:

"Elohim said, Behold, I have given you all seed-yielding herbs that are on the surface of the earth, and every tree that has seed-yielding fruit; to you it shall be for food. And for every animal of the earth, for every bird of the heaven, and for everything that creeps on the ground, in which there is a living spirit, all vegetational herbs shall be [their] food. And it was so". (BERESHIT 1:29-30)

RASHI [RABBI SHLOMO YITZCHAKI]:

❞ADAM and his wife were not permitted to kill any living thing and eat meat, but they could eat all vegetation".

THE RAMBAN [RABBI MOSHE BEN NACHMAN]:

❞Meat was not permitted until the time of NOAH as our sages note, and **this is the literal meaning of the text**. And the original prohibition to kill animals to eat their meat is because moving souls i.e. animals, have some extent of stature to their souls: they resemble intelligent souls i.e. man, and seek their [own] benefit and their food and run away from pain and death; and the verse states, **'Who knows the spirit of man whether it goes upward, and the spirit of the beast whether it goes downward to the earth?** - מִי יוֹדֵעַ רוּחַ בְּנֵי הָאָדָם הָעֹלָה הִיא לְמָעְלָה וְרוּחַ הַבְּהֵמָה הַיֹּרֶדֶת הִיא לְמַטָּה לָאָרֶץ' (ECCLESIASTES 3:21)".

RABBI DAVID ABUDRAHAM:

❞Regarding living creatures and the like, before eating them one does not say the blessing 'BOREH' which means 'create' (as one would recite 'BOREH PRI HA'ADAMA') for they were not created for this purpose, and the proof is that ADAM was not permitted to eat flesh... All of this is not repairing the creation; it is destroying and causing loss to the creation. We therefore do not say "BOREH" (on animal products)".

(ABUDARHAM, HILCHOT BERACHOT, 90)

RABBI YOSEF ALBO:

❝Aside from the intensive cruelty and anger involved in killing an animal, one accustoms themselves to the negative behavior of freely spilling blood. The consumption of flesh from living creatures gives birth to spiritual corpulence, murkiness and inflexibility of the soul... and because of this, even though the meat of some animals is considered good food and enjoyed by people, **GOD** wanted to remove the little bit of good one experiences when eating meat with the bad and massive damage that can come from it, so He forbade **ADAM** from eating animals❞.

(SEFER HA'IKARIM 3:15)

RABBI ISAAC BEN JUDAH ABARBANEL:

❝Therefore, at the beginning of creation when man was only allowed to consume vegetation and drink water their lifespan was longer. But when **NOAH** came and was allowed to eat meat and drink wine, life spans shrunk until where we are today❞.

(MA'AYANEI HAYESHU'AH, MA'AYAN 5, TAMAR 3)

❝This was because **ADAM** was in the **GARDEN OF EDEN**, a place of the choicest trees and fruit as the verse says (BERESHIT 2:9), 'God brought forth from the ground all trees beautiful to see and good to eat - וַיַּצְמַ֞ח יְהוָ֤ה אֱלֹהִים֙ מִן־הָ֣אֲדָמָ֔ה כָּל־עֵ֛ץ נֶחְמָ֥ד לְמַרְאֶ֖ה וְט֣וֹב לְמַאֲכָ֑ל'. And it says (BERESHIT 2:16), 'From all trees of the garden you will eat - מִכֹּ֥ל עֵֽץ־הַגָּ֖ן אָכֹ֥ל תֹּאכֵֽל'. But when **NOAH** and his sons exited the Ark, there was no vegetation nor did they have fruit of trees available. If they would wait until they had sowed fields and planted groves they would have starved to death. Therefore, they were permitted to eat meat".

(Abarbanel - Bereshit 9:1)

❙❙What seems most correct to me and the accurate interpretation is that **Adam** was forbidden to eat meat because he was spiritually complete, and **Noah** and his children were permitted to eat meat because of their evil nature and this interpretation implies that nourishment from vegetation is good and very appropriate [...] Whereas eating meat is quite the opposite; it brings out hot, boiling, red blood, it inclines one to cruelty, anger and overcoming another with malice. It easily rots and readies one for a quick death. Aside from all that is said with regard to killing a living creature, it also teaches cruelty and freely spilling blood.

God's desire was to straighten the path of the first man to direct him in righteousness and have him reach fulfillment. Therefore, He commanded him to take nourishment from vegetation which is more wholesome, i.e., from fruits and vegetation, but not to eat meat [...] But when 'the human population increased and became more morally degraded than their ancestors, their ways became corrupt - הֵחֵל הָאָדָם לָרֹב, וְהֵרֵעוּ מֵאֲבוֹתָם, וְהִשְׁחִית כָּל־בָּשָׂר אֶת־דַּרְכּוֹ' (Bereshit 6:1), even though they were eating vegetation and no meat; leading to the ultimate decree of their destruction in the generation of the flood. Almighty **GOD** saw that the good instructions He gave to men did not help them improve their ways; He therefore permitted **NOAH** and his progeny to eat meat.

It was as though He said: consume what you please from the vegetation or from meat, '**as the vegetation, I have now given to you everything** - כְּיֶרֶק עֵשֶׂב נָתַתִּי לָכֶם אֶת־כֹּל' (BERESHIT 9:3), because now their negative qualities could not be corrected through their way of eating, only by way of punishment".   (ABARBANEL - DEVARIM 14)

❙❙ 'But for your blood, for your souls, I will demand an account - וְאַךְ אֶת־דִּמְכֶם לְנַפְשֹׁתֵיכֶם אֶדְרֹשׁ' (BERESHIT 9:5) – When **GOD** gave permission to **NOAH** and his sons to eat flesh He said, 'But for the blood, for your souls, I will demand'. **GOD** was concerned that **cruelty and wickedness would develop within them as a result of eating meat, and they would eventually murder one another** [...] Because of this, the Prophet specifies that in the days of the **MESSIAH** both the lion and sheep will eat straw".   (ABARBANEL, ISAIAH 11)

THE MALBIM (RABBI MEIR LEIBUSH BEN YEHIEL MICHEL WISSER):

❙❙ At the time of the creation **GOD** did not give carnivorous animals permission to tear into living creatures and eat them [...] therefore, in the future when the world will be repaired, both the lion and cattle will eat straw; Man similarly was not permitted to eat meat.

It was only after the sin that the desire for meat was implanted in carnivorous animals as well as in man. However, researchers have shown that humans are not designed to eat meat, as we can see from the construction of our teeth and molars. Vegetarian animals by their nature are sustained by vegetation, and many people in India live from fruits and are of gentler nature".

(THE MALBIM ON BERESHIT 1:29)

❚❚ GOD permitted them to eat meat to prevent man from killing another, because all trees and vegetation of the field and all food was destroyed".   (THE MALBIM ON BERESHIT 9:1)

RABBI JACOB BEN ABBA MARI BEN SIMSON ANATOLI:

❚❚ Bread and water are necessary to prevent starvation and thirst, but wine and meat are not suitable for the sick, and for the healthy they are simply unnecessary. All THE TORAH stories are recounted for a reason. All of the generations before the flood lived the longest lives of anyone described in THE TORAH, and they were not given meat and wine; but after the flood it was given to them to experience though not to be consumed on a routine basis".   (MALMAD HA-TALMIDIM [=THE STUDENTS'

INSTRUCTION), PARASHAT BESHALACH, DIBBUR HAMATCHIL: ZE HADERECH)

RABBI YITZCHAK HEBENSTREIT:

❚❚ One should know, aside from the fact that it is inappropriate for man to eat meat due to tradition, ethics, religion and wisdom, it is also unnatural because man is unfit to eat meat as is proven by studying his organs. Man was created to live '**from the dews of heaven and the fat of the earth -** מִטַּל הַשָּׁמַיִם וּמִשְׁמַנֵּי הָאָרֶץ' (BERESHIT 27:28), from the grains and vegetation of the land and the fruits of the tree. All a person's organs indicate that we are not meat eaters.

All living things eat either vegetation or flesh and accordingly, The Master of Nature designed them to have differing digestive systems, body structures and organs.

We can also recognize that humans were not designed to eat meat because when we see a cow, sheep, goat or chickens and the like alive, there is no inner urge or desire to eat them. Likewise, raw meat does not raise within us any desire or appetite. Quite the contrary, it is disgusting and repulsive even to look at. It is only when meat is roasted, or cooked with vegetables, that we can consider eating it or tolerate its smell, and it is only the aroma of the vegetables and spices overpowering the odor of the meat. Only then does one's desire for meat arise, only when its smell, appearance and taste change, only when it is impossible to recognize that **it is a piece of dead flesh**.

But this is not the case with the natural tendency towards vegetables and fruits of the tree and the like. These produce strong natural feelings and call to us in a loving way: '**Wondrous to behold and good to eat -** נֶחְמָד לְמַרְאֶה וְטוֹב לְמַאֲכָל' (BERESHIT 2:9), and '**it is desirous to the eyes -** תַּאֲוָה־הוּא לָעֵינַיִם' (BERESHIT 3:6). **And the Prophet** says (Isaiah 28): 'While still in his hand, it is swallowed - בְּעוֹדָהּ בְּכַפּוֹ יִבְלָעֶנָּה'.

Man desires fruits so much that God needed to warn him, 'you should not stop learning because of them!' for **Rabbi Shimon** says (Pirkei Avot, chapter 3):

"If one is walking on the way and learning and interrupts his learning and says, 'how beautiful is this tree or how pleasant is this ploughed field', they bear guilt for their soul!"

A great desire awakens in their midst to taste the fruits and eat them fresh as they were created. Is this not enough proof that these are the natural foods for a person?

And since eating meat is unnatural for humans, it follows that eating meat damages and shortens one's life. It is understood that if one goes against nature it is impossible that nature will give them a pass and fill their days, for nature does not tolerate those who violate her; He does what he wants and she does what she wants; it is a silent but heavy war between them, until the measure is filled. Then nature will vomit them out of her, as it says in Tana Deve Eliyahu, I call the heavens and the Earth to be my witnesses that man was not created just to die and his problems only come as a result of gluttony and over-indulgence. And if you find one in a thousand people who eats meat and is healthy and lives long, this is extraordinary, and who knows if you will find someone like this, even one in a thousand! Most medical experts state in their books that all illnesses result from a meat-based diet, since it goes against nature. Likewise, all medicines are made from various plants in an attempt to align the sick person back with nature as the adage (RABBI YOCHANAN) in THE TALMUD says (BERACHOT 40):

'one who regularly consumes lentils prevents disease from his house, and mustard too prevents illness from his house'.

And they say (BERACHOT 44): **'leeks are beneficial for the intestine'** and we have seen and heard that when one eats what is intended for them they will feel no digestive pain. But after eating meat one experiences digestive difficulties because their system has not been built for eating meat but for vegetation".

(RABBI YITZCHAK HEBENSTREIT: BOOK KIVROTH HATTA'AVAH)

RABBI YOSEF DOV SOLOVEITCHIK:

❚❚ There is a distinct reluctance, almost an unwillingness, on the part of THE TORAH to grant man the privilege to consume meat. Man as an animal-eater is looked at askance by THE TORAH.

There are definitive vegetarian tendencies in the Bible... if we disregard conventional opinions and attempt to penetrate into the substrata of halachic philosophy, we will detect such ideas.

Paradoxically man has overreached himself, creating a new demand, a simple insistence upon something which by right does not belong to him, namely, life that is equal to his, flesh that is not different from his own, and he succeeded. **GOD**, as it were, gave in and compromised with man.

Is THE TORAH very happy about this? Somehow, we intuitively feel the silent tragic note that pervades the whole chapter. THE TORAH was compelled to admit defeat to human nature that was corrupted by man himself and willy-nilly approved the radical change in him.

Taking another's life became habitual for man. At once THE TORAH began to regulate the 'murder' of other lives, to restrict its practice by complicating the procedure.

CHAZAL formulated this tendency in their famous maxim: THE TORAH only provided for the evil inclination: it is better for the people of Israel to eat the flesh of animals that are ritually slaughtered than the flesh of animals that have perished (KIDDUSHIN 22)".

(RAV YOSEF DOV SOLOVEITCHIK / THE EMERGENCE OF ETHICAL MAN - MAN AS A CARNIVOROUS BEING)

THE PROHIBITION TO SACRIFICE OUTSIDE OF THE MISHKAN

אִישׁ אִישׁ מִבֵּית יִשְׂרָאֵל אֲשֶׁר יִשְׁחַט שׁוֹר אוֹ־כֶשֶׂב אוֹ־עֵז בַּמַּחֲנֶה אוֹ
אֲשֶׁר יִשְׁחַט מִחוּץ לַמַּחֲנֶה: וְאֶל־פֶּתַח אֹהֶל מוֹעֵד לֹא הֱבִיאוֹ לְהַקְרִיב
קָרְבָּן לַי־הֹוָה לִפְנֵי מִשְׁכַּן יְ־הֹוָה דָּם יֵחָשֵׁב לָאִישׁ הַהוּא דָּם שָׁפָךְ
וְנִכְרַת הָאִישׁ הַהוּא מִקֶּרֶב עַמּוֹ: ‏(ויקרא י"ז, ג'-ד')

"Each and every person of the House of Israel who will slaughter an ox, lamb, or goat within the encampment or who will slaughter [it] beyond the encampment. And to the entrance of the Tent of Meeting he did not bring it so that it may be brought as an offering to Adonay, before the Mishkan of Adonay; it shall be considered for that person as blood, he has spilled blood, and that person shall be cut off from among his people". (Vayikra 17:3-4)

Eating an animal was permitted only when offering it as a sacrifice in the Tabernacle. If one slaughtered an animal for a sacrifice but did not offer it in the Tabernacle, "it shall be considered for that person as blood, he has spilled blood - דָּם יֵחָשֵׁב לָאִישׁ הַהוּא דָּם שָׁפָךְ" (VAYIKRA 17:4), and he would deserve to be cut off of the Jewish nation (KARET).

THE TORAH text seems straightforward but there is a difference of opinion between **RABBI YISHMAEL** and **RABBI AKIVA**. **RAMBAN** explains this verse using its literal meaning which is in accord with the opinion of **RABBI YISHMAEL**, that the punishment of KARET befalls one who slaughtered an animal to eat but not for the purpose of sacrificing it in the Tabernacle, because the nation of Israel was not granted permission to eat meat for pleasure before they entered the land of Israel. This is the understanding of **RAMBAN**, **VILNA GAON**, **SFORNO**, **OHR HACHAYIM** and others.

Graves of Craving

וְהָאסַפְסֻף אֲשֶׁר בְּקִרְבּוֹ הִתְאַוּוּ תַּאֲוָה וַיָּשֻׁבוּ וַיִּבְכּוּ גַּם בְּנֵי יִשְׂרָאֵל
וַיֹּאמְרוּ מִי יַאֲכִלֵנוּ בָּשָׂר: (בְּמִדְבַּר י״א, ד׳)

"The collection [of nationalities] among them began
to have strong cravings, and Bnei Yisrael turned and
began to weep; and they said 'Who will feed us meat?'"

(BAMIDBAR 11:4)

The Lord then answered that He would give them meat, and added:

לֹא יוֹם אֶחָד תֹּאכְלוּן וְלֹא יוֹמָיִם וְלֹא | חֲמִשָּׁה יָמִים וְלֹא עֲשָׂרָה יָמִים
וְלֹא עֶשְׂרִים יוֹם: עַד | חֹדֶשׁ יָמִים עַד אֲשֶׁר־יֵצֵא מֵאַפְּכֶם וְהָיָה לָכֶם
לְזָרָא יַעַן כִּי־מְאַסְתֶּם אֶת־יְהֹוָה אֲשֶׁר בְּקִרְבְּכֶם ... : (בְּמִדְבַּר י״א, י״ט-כ׳)

"Not for one day will you be eating and not for two
days; not for five days, not for ten days, and not for
twenty days. But rather for a month of days, until it
comes out of your nostrils and it will be repulsive to
you; [this is] because you have rejected Adonay Who is
among you..."   (BAMIDBAR 11:19-20)

הַבָּשָׂר עוֹדֶנּוּ בֵּין שִׁנֵּיהֶם טֶרֶם יִכָּרֵת וְאַף יְהֹוָה חָרָה בָעָם וַיַּךְ יְהֹוָה
בָּעָם מַכָּה רַבָּה מְאֹד: וַיִּקְרָא אֶת־שֵׁם־הַמָּקוֹם הַהוּא קִבְרוֹת הַתַּאֲוָה
... :
(בְּמִדְבַּר י״א, ל״ג-ל״ד)

"The meat was still between their teeth before it was
[even] finished, when the wrath of Adonay was incited
upon the people, and Adonay smote the people an
enormous blow. He called the name of that place Kivrot
Hata'avah..."   (BAMIDBAR 11:33-34)

THE RADAK, RABBI DAVID son of YOSEF KIMCHI expounds:

❙❙ 'They tested God in their hearts - וַיְנַסּוּ־אֵל בִּלְבָבָם'.

Their plot was to test GOD by requesting meat, for
the MANNA was good and pleasing food and they did not
need the meat, but they wanted to test Him. But they
did not articulate this. They said 'we need the meat' and
denigrated the MANNA, saying (BAMIDBAR 11:6) 'Our bodies
are dried out, for there is nothing at all; we have
nothing but manna to look at - נַפְשֵׁנוּ יְבֵשָׁה אֵין כֹּל בִּלְתִּי אֶל־

הַמָּן עֵינֵינוּ', and then followed this with (Bamidbar 21:5) 'We are disgusted with this rotten bread - וְנַפְשֵׁנוּ קָצָה בַּלֶּחֶם הַקְּלֹקֵל'. They were asking for food to fulfill their desire, as he said (Bamidbar 11:4): 'Began to have strong cravings - הִתְאַוּוּ תַּאֲוָה. And he said 'To their souls - לְנַפְשָׁם' (Psalms 18:18), for the soul is the cause of lust, as it says (Devarim 12:20): 'If you desire to eat meat - כִּי־תְאַוֶּה נַפְשְׁךָ לֶאֱכֹל בָּשָׂר'.

(Rabbi David Kimchi, HaRadak, Psalms 78:18)

Rabbi Isaac ben Judah Abarbanel explains in his commentary regarding the MANNA:

❙❙ God said to Moshe: meat is not a necessity but rather a matter of gluttony, to fill their stomachs and satisfy their base desires'. Moreover, meat brings out in a person malicious and cruel blood, and because of this you will find that the carnivorous animals and birds that eat meat are cruel and evil. But sheep, cattle, chickens and pigeons, who live from vegetation, do not act in a cruel or evil manner. For this reason, the Prophet prophesied that in the time of the coming redemption 'Both the lion and cattle will eat hay - אַרְיֵה כַּבָּקָר יֹאכַל־תֶּבֶן'. And the rationale is that 'They shall neither harm nor destroy - לֹא־יָרֵעוּ וְלֹא־יַשְׁחִיתוּ' etc. Thus God did not say to Moshe that He would give them meat, but rather bread, for this is nourishment that is pleasant and necessary and consistent with the nature of man, hence 'I am going to rain down for you bread from heaven - הִנְנִי מַמְטִיר לָכֶם לֶחֶם מִן־הַשָּׁמָיִם".

(Abarbanel - Shemot 16)

RABBI SHABBETHAI BEN JOSEPH BASS:

❯❯ Why does the text say 'Prepare yourselves - הִתְקַדְּשׁוּ'?
It should have simply said, 'Say unto the people ... tomorrow you will eat meat - וְאֶל־הָעָם תֹּאמַר ... לְמָחָר וַאֲכַלְתֶּם בָּשָׂר'. Additionally, what preparation do you need for eating? The answer is that this refers to the negative unfolding of events written at the end, which came upon them as a result of their eating the meat".

(SIFTEI CHACHAMIM, BAMIDBAR 11)

THE MALBIM (RABBI MEIR LEIBUSH BEN YEHIEL MICHEL WISSER):

❯❯ We do not require actual meat and fish to experience palatal pleasure, because whenever we want to taste fish all we need to do is remember the fish that we ate in Egypt, and we can experience the same sensation again. However, our request for meat is to benefit our body's health by eating meat. Recalling the tastes of fish in Egypt does not help us at all, and is as futile as recalling 'the squash and watermelon - אֵת הַקִּשֻּׁאִים וְאֵת הָאֲבַטִּחִים'. Just recalling the taste of fish and meat they had while eating MANNA is for naught, because actual meat would not be in their stomachs".

(THE MALBIM - BAMIDBAR 11)

OHR HACHAYIM, [RABBI CHAYIM BEN ATAR]:

❯❯ Because **GOD** acted severely with those cravers who wanted to eat meat in the desert (BAMIDBAR 11) and those cravers were buried, since then craving for meat was forbidden. Concerning this it says, 'when God widens your boundary... and you will say - כִּי־יַרְחִיב יְ־הֹוָה אֱ־לֹהֶיךָ אֶת־גְּבֻלְךָ ... וְאָמַרְתָּ' ["I will eat meat"]... the understanding of this text is that even when you explicitly state that you wish to consume meat, echoing the words of those cravers who asked, 'who will feed us meat? - מִי יַאֲכִלֵנוּ בָּשָׂר'. THE TORAH also says, 'when your soul craves - כִּי־תְאַוֶּה נַפְשְׁךָ', which strongly hints to the words used regarding those cravers in the desert about whom the verse states that 'They had strong cravings - הִתְאַוּוּ תַּאֲוָה'. Still, THE TORAH permits this and states, 'You may eat meat according to your craving - בְּכָל־אַוַּת נַפְשְׁךָ תֹּאכַל בָּשָׂר'".

(OHR HaChayim - Devarim ch. 12)

"And you will say, I will eat meat"

כִּי־יַרְחִיב יְ־הֹוָה אֱ־לֹהֶיךָ אֶת־גְּבֻלְךָ כַּאֲשֶׁר דִּבֶּר־לָךְ וְאָמַרְתָּ אֹכְלָה בָשָׂר כִּי־תְאַוֶּה נַפְשְׁךָ לֶאֱכֹל בָּשָׂר בְּכָל־אַוַּת נַפְשְׁךָ תֹּאכַל בָּשָׂר: כִּי־יִרְחַק מִמְּךָ הַמָּקוֹם אֲשֶׁר יִבְחַר יְ־הֹוָה אֱ־לֹהֶיךָ לָשׂוּם שְׁמוֹ שָׁם וְזָבַחְתָּ מִבְּקָרְךָ וּמִצֹּאנְךָ אֲשֶׁר נָתַן יְ־הֹוָה לְךָ כַּאֲשֶׁר צִוִּיתִךָ וְאָכַלְתָּ בִּשְׁעָרֶיךָ בְּכֹל אַוַּת נַפְשֶׁךָ: אַךְ כַּאֲשֶׁר יֵאָכֵל אֶת־הַצְּבִי וְאֶת־הָאַיָּל כֵּן תֹּאכְלֶנּוּ הַטָּמֵא וְהַטָּהוֹר יַחְדָּו יֹאכְלֶנּוּ:

(דְּבָרִים י"ב, כ'-כ"ב)

"When Adonay, your God, expands your border as He promised you, and you say, "I would like to eat meat" because you have an appetite to eat meat; to the full extent of your appetite eat meat. When the place is distant from you that Adonay, your God, chooses to set His Presence there, you may slaughter some of your cattle or your flocks that Adonay gave you, as I have commanded you; and you will eat in your cities with all your appetite. Only, as the dear and the gazelle may be eaten, so may you eat it; the ritually unclean and the clean together may eat it. (DEVARIM 12:20-22)

These verses indicate that from the moment Israel entered the land, they were permitted to eat meat. However, the permission granted in these verses puts the consumption of meat in a negative light and links it to a base desire. We shall bring our sages thoughts on the nature of this permission.

CHULLIN 84A:

❙❙ THE TORAH taught that a person should only consume meat in that manner (i.e. by hunting). In a similar vein, the sages taught in a Baraita that THE TORAH verse stating: **'When the Lord, your God, expands your boundary -** כִּי־יַרְחִיב יְ־הֹוָה אֱ־לֹהֶיךָ אֶת־גְּבֻלְךָ' (DEVARIM 12:20) means that it is a desired mode of behavior that a person should consume meat only to satiate his appetite (i.e. when his desire overcomes him)".

The Baraita continues:

❙❙ One might have thought that a person may purchase meat from the marketplace and consume it. However, the next verse states: **'And you may slaughter of your cattle and of your flock -** וְזָבַחְתָּ מִבְּקָרְךָ וּמִצֹּאנְךָ' indicating that one should only consume the meat of animals of his own flock. One might have thought that a person may slaughter all of his cattle, and consume the meat. Therefore, the verse states: 'Of your cattle - מִבְּקָרְךָ' indicating some, but not all of, your cattle".

RASHI [RABBI SHLOMO YITZCHAKI] (Chullin 84a) explains:

❚❚ 'Of your cattle - מִבְּקָרְךָ' – one can take from their flock, but if they do not have any, one should not go to the market and buy meat".

BA'AL HATURIM [RABBI YAAKOV BEN ASHER] (DEVARIM 12:20):

❚❚ 'Eat meat - תֹּאכַל בָּשָׂר' – the adjacent verse states, 'if it is distant from you - כִּי־יִרְחַק', intimating that one should distance themselves from eating meat, as is stated in the chapter (CHULLIN 84A) entitled, 'covering the blood'".

RABBI SHABBATAI HAKOHEN [THE SHACH]:

❚❚ THE TORAH taught that one may not eat meat until after their boundaries are widened – i.e. they are not poor but rather economically stable and stating, 'I will eat meat - וְאָמַרְתָּ אֹכְלָה בָשָׂר'. The craving then follows as written in the text, 'because you desire - כִּי־תְאַוֶּה נַפְשְׁךָ'. Still, THE TORAH does not permit the consumption of meat until the craving has completely overtaken the individual, as described in the text, 'according to your desire you may eat meat - בְּכָל־אַוַּת נַפְשְׁךָ תֹּאכַל בָּשָׂר'. You are no better than ADAM HARISHON, who never ate meat in his life".

(SIFTEI KOHEN AL HATORAH, PAASHAT RE'EH)

RABBEINU BACHA'YE BEN ASHER:

❝ The animal soul (within man) is the drive to eat and drink, copulate and sleep and express hatred and anger. These drives are common both to man and to animals, and it resides in the liver and is termed 'the mind and spirit', as is written (DEVARIM 12:20): **'if you desire to eat meat - כִּי־תְאַוֶּה נַפְשְׁךָ לֶאֱכֹל בָּשָׂר'**. And it is written (ECCLESIASTES 7:9) **'Be not hasty to become angry - "אַל־תְּבַהֵל בְּרוּחֲךָ לִכְעוֹס".**

(RABENU BECHA'YE - BERESHIT 2:7)

RABBI AVRAHAM IBN EZRA:

❝ There are two powers. In the holy language they are generally referred to as spirit (RU'ACH) and soul (NEFESH), as the soul is the place of wisdom and it resides in the brain… and the soul resides in the liver and it is that which drives the desire to eat, thus it is written, **'when your soul craves - "כִּי־תְאַוֶּה נַפְשֶׁךָ".** (IBN EZRA - SHEMOT 23:25)

RAV YAAKOV, SON OF CHANANEL SKILEE (a student of the RASHBA):

❝ Note how much THE TORAH warns us against cravings and that we should distance ourselves from them and not submit to them unless in great need, as is written (DEVARIM 12:20) **'when you crave to eat meat - כִּי־תְאַוֶּה נַפְשְׁךָ לֶאֱכֹל בָּשָׂר',** which is to say that when you desire meat — do not eat it on a regular basis but rather wait for the appropriate time, specifically **'when God has widened your boundaries - כִּי־יַרְחִיב יְהוָֹה אֱ־לֹהֶיךָ אֶת־גְּבוּלְךָ',** i.e., after the land has been conquered with great effort, resulting in greater cravings. And when you eat meat it should be in small amounts and from that which you have and own as the verse states, **'from your cattle and sheep - מִבְּקָרְךָ וּמִצֹּאנְךָ'**, meaning only a part of your flock, not the entirety may be consumed. All of these restrictions are to distance us from the cravings which lead to death. Take heed from the Wayward Son as his misdeed is gluttonously consuming meat and wine, and THE TORAH assigns him to death by stoning".

(TORAT HAMINCHA, PARASHAT NASO, DERASHAH 55, DIBBUR HAMATCHIL: HALO TIR'EH)

⫿ And he said that the 'broken spirit' refers to the mixed multitude who were drawn by passion and craving to the sacrifices of alien Gods. The text implies that this actually means that their desire was to consume meat, for the verse states (DEVARIM 12): **'when you crave to eat meat - כִּי־תְאַוֶּה נַפְשְׁךָ לֶאֱכֹל בָּשָׂר'**, and as the verse states, **'If sheep and cattle were slaughtered for them, would it suffice for them? If all the fish of the sea were gathered for them, would it suffice for them? - הֲצֹאן וּבָקָר יִשָּׁחֵט לָהֶם וּמָצָא לָהֶם אִם אֶת־כָּל־דְּגֵי הַיָּם יֵאָסֵף לָהֶם'** And another similar verse, **'But the multitude among them began to have strong cravings - וְהָאסַפְסֻף אֲשֶׁר בְּקִרְבּוֹ הִתְאַוּוּ תַּאֲוָה'**. Meditate on this".

(TORAT HAMINCHA, PARASHAT BEHA'ALOTCHA, DERASHAH 56, DIBBUR HAMATCHIL: DAVAR ACHER, ZIVCHEI ELOKIM RUACH NISHBARA)

❙❙ There is a sin committed with the mouth of consuming forbidden foods and it is caused by craving. When the craving overcomes an individual, they desire that which is forbidden, and when a questionable item comes to their attention they will rationalize and validate it. Therefore, one should distance themselves from cravings. Consider how THE TORAH warns us about eating meat (DEVARIM 12:20) 'When your soul craves to eat meat ... with all your desire you will eat - ... כִּי־תְאַוֶּה נַפְשְׁךָ לֶאֱכֹל בָּשָׂר בְּכָל־אַוַּת נַפְשְׁךָ תֹּאכַל בָּשָׂר'. Consider the punishment for one who has overeaten like the Wayward Son, and as KING SOLOMON said in his wisdom (PROVERBS 21:25) 'The cravings of a lazy man will bring about his death - תַּאֲוַת עָצֵל תְּמִיתֶנּוּ'. And when we consider our need to eat and its purpose, it is only to provide for our physical needs. More than that is excessive and wastes money and one's body and soul. Therefore, one should distance themselves and beware of the cravings of this world, and by doing so will fulfill their purpose and avoid eating forbidden foods".

(TORAT HAMINCHA, ROSH HASHANA, DERASHAH 77, DIBBUR HAMATCHIL: VEYESH AVERAH)

RABBI NAFTALI ZVI YEHUDA BERLIN, THE NETZIV FROM VOLOZHIN:

❙❙ 'And you will say, I will eat meat ... you'll sacrifice from your cattle - וְאָמַרְתָּ אֹכְלָה בָשָׂר ... וְזָבַחְתָּ מִבְּקָרְךָ'. This is a negative commandment implied by a positive one. i.e. to not eat without ritual slaughtering".

(HA'AMEK DAVAR, DEVARIM 17:14)

Rabbi Menachem Mendel of Kotzk:

❙❙Why is a person not permitted to eat meat on the first nine days of the month of Av? Is it not the case that a person is not permitted to eat meat all year round?"

(Emet Ve'Emunah, letter 336)

Rabbi Shlomo Kluger:

❙❙They never would have been granted permission to partake of lustful meat if not for their deep desire for which there was no cure: were it not for this they would have never consumed meat. Since sacrifices were nonexistent at that time, they would not have been able to overcome their craving. As a result of their powerful craving, meat was permitted, just as the captive woman was permitted. As the verse states (Devarim 12:20), 'when God widens your boundary... you will say: I will eat meat - כִּי־יַרְחִיב יְהוָֹה אֱ־לֹהֶיךָ אֶת־גְּבוּלְךָ כַּאֲשֶׁר דִּבֶּר־לָךְ וְאָמַרְתָּ אֹכְלָה בָשָׂר'. Meat should have most certainly been forbidden, but only because 'when you crave to eat meat - כִּי־תְאַוֶּה נַפְשְׁךָ לֶאֱכֹל בָּשָׂר בְּכָל־אַוַּת נַפְשֶׁךָ', implying that due to the great desire for which there is no cure, only because of that craving, you may 'eat meat - תֹּאכַל בָּשָׂר'.

(Kehilat Yaakov, Elul, Drush 20, page 193)

Maharal of Prague [Rabbi Judah Loew ben Bezalel]:

❙❙The term 'craving - תַּאֲוָה' refers to the totally physical desire just as we find in the verse (Bamidbar 11:4): 'But the multitude among them began to have strong cravings -

'וְהָאספְסֵף אֲשֶׁר בְּקִרְבּוֹ הִתְאַוּוּ תַאֲוָה' (Devarim 12:20); 'When you crave to eat meat - כִּי־תְאַוֶּה נַפְשְׁךָ לֶאֱכֹל בָּשָׂר' (Bereshit 3:6); 'it was a craving (i.e., delight) to the eyes - וְכִי תַאֲוָה־הוּא לָעֵינַיִם'. and 'lust - תַּאֲוָה' will never be found only in this matter".

(Tiferet Israel, chapter 45)

Rabbi Shlomo Ephrayim from Luntshitz (Author of the Torah commentary: Keli Yekar):

❝ This will lead to the removal of the veil of shame (and acting in a decent manner) from your face till you clearly say 'I shall eat meat - אֹכְלָה בָשָׂר' – and this is not unlike one casting off the yoke of Heaven.

[…] all day you will deeply lust and you will not feel any shame for proclaiming that you desire meat. I permit this to you by means of 'sacrificing your cattle…as I have commanded you - וְזָבַחְתָּ מִבְּקָרְךָ וְגוֹ'. כַּאֲשֶׁר צִוִּיתִךָ'. not to partake in it on a regular basis, but only when the craving overcomes you. Thus, the verse states (Devarim 12:22), 'But as the deer and the gazelle are eaten, so may you eat them - אַךְ כַּאֲשֶׁר יֵאָכֵל אֶת־הַצְּבִי וְאֶת־הָאַיָּל כֵּן תֹּאכְלֶנּוּ' and as it says (Vayikra 17:13), 'who traps a wild animal or bird - אֲשֶׁר יָצוּד צֵיד חַיָּה אוֹ־עוֹף'.

Our Rabbis have stated (Chullin 84a): 'The Torah taught that a person should consume meat only with this mode of preparation. This means that if one becomes habituated to eating the animals they own, 'a bull, sheep or goat - שׁוֹר אוֹ־כֶשֶׂב אוֹ־עֵז' (Vayikra 17:3), then they will crave and become accustomed to eating meat all the time.

However, if one must hunt in the forests and deserts for an animal and encounter resistance, danger and difficulty, then their craving will diminish, because the pleasure of eating the animal will not be worth the effort and difficulty [...] therefore THE TORAH says (DEVARIM 12:22), 'But as the deer and the gazelle are eaten, so may you eat them - אַךְ כַּאֲשֶׁר יֵאָכֵל אֶת־הַצְּבִי וְאֶת־הָאַיָּל כֵּן תֹּאכְלֶנּוּ'.

The intent: it is upon this condition that you are allowed to eat meat: you should not become accustomed to eating the deer and gazelle. Naturally, one would not be accustomed to eating them because they are wild animals and need to be trapped, and due to the effort involved one does not often eat them – so should all meat be eaten, only seldom".   (KELI YEKAR, DEVARIM 12:20)

▌▌'And hunt game for me - וְצוּדָה לִּי (צידה) צַיִד' (BERESHIT 27:3) - Why did YITZCHAK request something that needed to be hunted? Didn't he have an animal in his flock which tasted like deer? Did he need to send his son out to the place of animal herds? It seems obvious to me THE TORAH is teaching us the way to perceive meat – as our sages said (CHULLIN 84A): 'If he hunts an animal or a bird - אֲשֶׁר יָצוּד צֵיד חַיָּה אוֹ־עוֹף' (VAYIKRA 17:3), meaning that we should not see it as being easily accessible so that consuming meat does not become a routine. As the verse says (DEVARIM 12:20): 'according to your desire you may eat. But as the deer and the gazelle are eaten, so you may eat them - בְּכָל־אַוַּת נַפְשְׁךָ תֹּאכַל בָּשָׂר ... אַךְ כַּאֲשֶׁר יֵאָכֵל אֶת־הַצְּבִי

'וְאֶת־הָאַיָּל כֵּן תֹאכְלֶנּוּ' implying that meat should be eaten at non-fixed intervals as opposed to being consumed on a regular basis. Just as the deer and the gazelle are not found in one's home as they are wild, undomesticated animals living in the deserts and forests, they are seldom eaten due to their ability to avoid traps and capture. As a consequence of being rarely caught, they are rarely eaten by people – this helps a person not become accustomed to regularly eating meat. Consuming meat gives rise to cruel and negative tendencies in the individual. All carnivorous birds eat flesh and likewise the lion thrashes its prey and eats it, therefore it is prophesized (ISAIAH 11:7): **'A lion like cattle will eat straw -** וְאַרְיֵה כַּבָּקָר יֹאכַל־תֶּבֶן' [i.e., in the days of the Messiah], for there will be peace in the world between all living things. Therefore **YITZCHAK** said (BERESHIT 27:3), **'Go hunt for me -** צָיִד (צידה) וְצוּדָה לִי', because he wanted to consume meat with the proper mindset and consideration".

(KELI YEKAR, BERESHIT 27:3)

RABBI YITZCHAK HEBENSTREIT:

❙❙ A habit becomes one's nature. Since it was difficult to separate and distance them from consuming dead flesh, when **GOD** saw that prohibiting the act would not help, He allowed it. **THE TORAH** speaks with regard to people who crave as specified in THE TORAH (DEVARIM 12:20): **'When the Lord, your God, expands your boundary, and you say, 'I will eat meat... because you desire to eat meat, you may eat meat, according to your desire -**

כִּי־יַרְחִיב יְהֹוָה אֱ־לֹהֶיךָ אֶת־גְּבֻלְךָ ... וְאָמַרְתָּ אֹכְלָה בָשָׂר כִּי־תְאַוֶּה נַפְשְׁךָ לֶאֱכֹל בָּשָׂר בְּכָל־אַוַּת נַפְשְׁךָ תֹּאכַל בָּשָׂר'. It is obvious that THE TORAH speaks to the people who crave, for had He not permitted it, they would eat it anyway against His will. This is akin to the law of the captive woman who is permitted to be taken in war, where our scholars say that by permitting this THE TORAH is actually appeasing the evil inclination. For had GOD not permitted it, she would have been taken against His will. We see our scholars speak with denigration of THE SHOCHET (slaughterer) when they say (KIDDUSHIN 22) 'Even the best butcher is a partner of AMALEK'.

'This is because the guilty prey upon the guilty. This is this reason for the established HALACHA (REMA, SHULCHAN ARUCH, YOREH DE'AH, SIMAN 28) that we do not make the blessing Shehecheyanu when slaughtering because we are harming a living being, and the verse states (PSALMS 10:3), **'the robber congratulates himself for having blasphemed the Lord -** וּבֹצֵעַ בֵּרֵךְ נִאֵץ | יְהֹוָה'. It is from the permission given to eat meat that one learns the prohibition; from the 'yes' we learn the 'no'. The bread requested from GOD was asked for properly, as it is good and fitting and needed for survival. Therefore, it was given to them regularly, every day in the morning with a bright and cheery face. It is clear as day that bread is important sustenance, and they did not request it to fulfill their craving; not so for meat which comes from murder and cruelty and one can live without it. Therefore, it was improper that they requested meat and it was given to them improperly, with a darkened and angry face. Since eating meat has four periods in THE TORAH, alternatively, twice forbidden and twice permitted; and even when eating it was permitted, the permission to eat it was not total, therefore it was delivered to them in the evening, specifically at a time that is not day nor night, a time when the light and dark are mixed, just like meat whose prohibition and permission are interwoven. It is from here that THE TORAH teaches us ways of decency; that a person should eat meat only in the evening because truly, one should never eat meat. Only when their craving overcomes them, even then they should restrict themselves to only eating it in the evening, the time that is neither day nor night, reminding the eater that eating meat is not forbidden nor is it permitted. Moreover, they should be cognizant that their eating is not consistent with the will of **GOD** and it is possible that by eating with this mindset one will find a way to stop this behavior, 'for he who confesses and forsakes sin will find mercy". (RABBI YITZCHAK HEBENSTREIT: BOOK KIVROTH HATTA'AVAH)

RABBI CHAYIM DAVID HALEVI:

❚❚The truth is that there is no conflict at all between Veganism and Judaism and it most certainly does not clash with HALACHA. Note that meat was forbidden to the first man, and it was only permitted to **NOAH** and onward, but after the giving of THE TORAH many animals were forbidden and only a few were permitted; but this is not the place to discuss this fundamental fact. Moreover, meat was only permitted due to the evil inclination, as it says (Devarim 12:20), 'When you crave to eat meat - כִּי־תְאַוֶּה נַפְשְׁךָ לֶאֱכֹל בָּשָׂר' (Chullin 84a), see the **Baal Ha'Ikarim**, stating that meat was permitted to be eaten only out of dire necessity (3rd article, chapter 15)". (Responsa Aseh Lecha Rav 5:47)

Rav Abraham Yitzchak Kook:

▌▌'And thou shalt say: I will eat meat, because you desire to eat meat; you may eat meat as you desire וְאָמַרְתָּ אֹכְלָה בָשָׂר כִּי־תְאַוֶּה נַפְשְׁךָ לֶאֱכֹל בָּשָׂר בְּכָל־אַוַּת נַפְשְׁךָ - תֹּאכַל בָּשָׂר' (Devarim 12:20). This is a subtle 'wise man's rebuke' disguised as a vague remark [...] The explicit explanation of this is that when the time comes for the human moral state to deplore [the consumption of] animal meat because it is morally repugnant, then you will not have the urge to eat meat and you will not eat it. The general rule for interpreting the Torah is that positive statements can be derived from negative statements, and negative statements can be derived from positive ones".

"The commandment to cover the blood of the animal or the bird is like a heavenly protest, which is confronted with the provisional authorization tied to the shameful state of man's soul, 'For the inclination of man's heart is evil from his youth - כִּי יֵצֶר לֵב הָאָדָם רַע מִנְּעֻרָיו' (Bereshit 8:21), and he says (Devarim 12:20), 'I will eat meat, because I desire to eat meat - אֹכְלָה בָשָׂר כִּי־תְאַוֶּה ... לֶאֱכֹל בָּשָׂר'. It is also the soul (Nefesh) that actually eats meat whenever it feels the urge because it lacks even the concept of internal restraint which would come from an understanding of the concepts of benevolence and justice. Therefore, THE TORAH commands: cover the blood to hide your shame and weak sense of justice [...] in order that you might become wiser and refine your sensibilities and realize that it is not appropriate to take the life of another living-sentient being to fulfill a physical need or an urge. Fulfillment of the heavenly directives and commandments produces a moral readiness and this potential can be realized when its time comes [...]'.

But my dear human, listen to the voice of **GOD** behind you calling loudly (SHEMOT 23:19): **'You must not cook a young animal in the milk of its mother - לֹא־תְבַשֵּׁל גְּדִי בַּחֲלֵב אִמּוֹ'** No! the sheep's primary purpose is not to be eaten with your sharp teeth or pluck its meat from the bone. And the milk is certainly not for your cooking purposes to fulfill your base cravings. Be aware that meat and milk are so far away from being considered food- it is disgusting to the point of being forbidden to be cooked or eaten together. Animals were not created for your consumptive pleasure and the milk was meant to be nourishment for whom nature intended, just as the milk from your mother's breast was assured to you when you were nursed".

(RABBI AVRAHAM YITZCHAK KOOK, THE VISION OF VEGETARIANISM AND PEACE) ❧❧

SUMMARY OF THE PROHIBITION VS PERMISSION OF MEAT CONSUMPTION IN **THE TORAH**

BERESHIT 1:29

The first will of the Creator: **PLANT-BASED FOOD.** MEAT CONSUMPTION WAS PROHIBITED.

....

BERESHIT 9:3

After the flood, after all living beings had transgressed and corrupted their ways on earth, MEAT CONSUMPTION RECEIVED A SHAMEFUL APPROVAL.

....

VAYIKRA 17:3-7

After the exodus from Egypt, MEAT CONSUMPTION WAS PERMITTED ONLY IN THE TABERNACLE following animal sacrifice, and was not permitted outside THE TEMPLE. ANY OTHER MEAT CONSUMPTION WAS PROHIBITED.

....

DEVARIM 12:20-22

When the people of Israel entered the Land of Israel, MEAT CONSUMPTION WAS PERMITTED EVEN OUTSIDE OF THE TEMPLE UNDER VERY LIMITED CIRCUMSTANCES: only infrequently and irregularly, like deer and gazelle are eaten – i.e., MEAT CONSUMPTION RECEIVED A SHAMEFUL APPROVAL.

Rabbi Yosef Albo understands the shameful legalization of meat consumption a posteriori, as follows:

❚❚When the Torah was given to Israel [...] even what it permitted to them was only to counteract the evil inclination, as it permitted them to [take a] beautiful captive woman [by force in war]".

(Sefer Ha'Ikarim 3:15)

Rabbi Yehudah HaChassid:

❚❚There are some actions permitted by the Torah, but if one should commit them they will be judged accordingly. For one must consider that the permission granted by the Torah is solely to battle the evil inclination, as in the case of the captured woman".

(Sefer Chasidim, siman 378)

Rav Yaakov, son of Chananel Skilee (one of the Rashba's students):

❚❚The Torah reveals to us another foundational principle: to distance ourselves from base desires which lead man to his death in this and the next world, as is written (Proverbs 21:25): 'The cravings of a lazy man will bring about his death - תַּאֲוַת עָצֵל תְּמִיתֶנּוּ'. The Torah has warned against this numerous times as is written (Devarim 12:20) 'Because you have an appetite to eat meat; to the full extent of your appetite eat meat - כִּי־תְאַוֶּה נַפְשְׁךָ לֶאֱכֹל בָּשָׂר בְּכָל־אַוַּת נַפְשְׁךָ תֹּאכַל בָּשָׂר' and many other such verses, as it is written (Proverbs 30:20): 'This is the way of an adulterous woman - כֵּן דֶּרֶךְ אִשָּׁה מְנָאָפֶת' since the

Torah views craving as it does an adulterous woman; for the adulterous woman eagerly walks the path of prostitutes and this is the nature of the animalistic soul".

(Torat HaMincha, Parashat Emor, Derashah 49, Dibbur HaMatchil: Od Toellet)

The words of **Rabbi Avraham Yitzchak Kook:**

❙❙So long as man is filled with base instincts and low morals, focused on filling their cruel desires upon living creatures to spill their blood and to swallow their bodies, there is no hope at all that the wild beast within the human will improve its way and cease spilling the blood of his friend".

(Rabbi Shimon Glitzenstein. A group of memoirs on Rabbi Avraham Yitzchak HaCohen Kook, Jerusalem. Otzar HaSefarim, 5733/1973)

ABRAHAM asked **MALKIZEDEK**: 'Based on what merit did you manage to last in the Ark, during the flood?'

Answered **MALKIZEDEK**, 'It was due to the righteousness that we did there'.

ABRAHAM asked, 'What act of righteousness did you perform on the ark? Were there poor people? Only **NOAH** and his children were there! Upon whom did you bestow righteousness?'

Answered **MALKIZEDEK**, 'Upon the animals and beasts and birds. We did not sleep, all night. We were always feeding and taking care of this one and that one, the entire night'".

(MIDRASH TEHILIM SHOCHER TOV, MIZMOR 37)

THE **PURPOSE** OF SACRIFICES

Those of the opinion that eating meat and spilling animals' blood is consistent with the will of **GOD**, often draw their proof from the commandant to bring sacrifices, and indeed, THE TORAH deals with this quite a lot. In the coming chapter we will bring our sages' commentary regarding the commandment to sacrifice.

MAIMONIDES opens chapter 32 of the Guide for the Perplexed (MOREH NEVUCHIM), with a biological claim: every living animal develops gradually, over time and space.

MAIMONIDES describes (there) how the malleable nerve becomes a tough tendon and generalizes the principle:

> For a sudden transition from one opposite to another is impossible. And therefore man, according to his nature, is not capable of abandoning suddenly all to which he was accustomed".

According to **Maimonides**, animal sacrifice was necessitated by the need for a gradual transition from a world of idolatry to a world governed by the true worship of **God**. He writes (There):

> ❚❚ And at that time the way of life generally accepted and customary in the whole world, and the universal service upon which we were brought up, consisted in offering various species of living beings in THE TEMPLES in which images were set up, in worshipping the latter, and in burning incense before them [...] **God**'s wisdom, may He be exalted, and His gracious cunning, which is manifest in regard to all His creatures, did not require that He give us a Law prescribing the rejection, abandonment, and abolition of all these kinds of worship. For at that time one could not conceive the acceptance of [such a Law], considering the nature of man, which always likes that to which he is accustomed [...] Therefore He, may He be exalted, allowed the abovementioned kinds of worship to remain, but transferred them from man-made or imaginary and unreal things to His own name".

This means that animal sacrifice was intended to help the Israelites to abandon idol worship. Given that at that time the entire world was accustomed to worshipping their idols with animal sacrifice, the Israelites were unwilling to accept a religion that did not require sacrifices. For this reason, **God** instructed the Israelites to sacrifice to Him rather than to idols.

Maimonides carries on the conversation to ask what would have happened had God commanded that He be worshipped not by way of sacrifice:

> ❙❙ At that time this would have been similar to the appearance of a Prophet in these times who, calling upon the people to worship **GOD**, would say: 'GOD has given you a law forbidding you to pray to Him, to fast, or to call upon Him for help in misfortune. Your worship should consist solely of meditation without any action or movement'".

Of course, we would not accept the words of such a Prophet. Similarly, says **MAIMONIDES**, the People of Israel would not have accepted THE TORAH if it had not commanded sacrifices. According to **MAIMONIDES**, the detailed laws of sacrifice are actually intended to distance us from idolatry and to limit its practice:

> ❙❙ For one kind of worship – I mean the offering of sacrifices – even though it was offered to His name, may He be exalted, was not prescribed to us in the way it existed at first, i.e., in such a way that sacrifices could be offered in every place and at every time. Nor could a Temple be set up in any time and place [...] On the contrary, He forbade all this and established one single house [THE TEMPLE] [...] so that sacrifices should not be offered elsewhere [...] Also only the offspring of one particular family can be Priest. All this was intended to decrease this kind of worship, so that only the portion of it should subsist whose abolition would not be wise, according to His wisdom".

Sacrifice is merely a means to a cause, a secondary intention. In this sense it is very much unlike other religious obligations such as prayer, which are closer to the initial intention.

According to **MAIMONIDES**, prayer and the like are only a means directed toward an end – which is devoutness, or cleaving to the Divine; and still they are closer to the first intention. On the other hand, sacrifice is a more distant means toward the end, and one in which there is very little of the holiness of the divine commandment. Its real purpose is to distance mankind from the sin of performing idolatrous ritual sacrifice.

Some might conclude from the many details of the laws pertaining to sacrifice how important and holy it is. **MAIMONIDES** counters this understanding and explains that the purpose of this excessive detail is to minimize the importance attributed to this form of worship and to accustom man to the practice and distance him from idol worship.

MAIMONIDES brings the admonishments of the Prophets against Israel for narrowing their focus to worshipping in the form of sacrifice:

וַיֹּאמֶר שְׁמוּאֵל הַחֵפֶץ לַי־הֹוָה בְּעֹלוֹת וּזְבָחִים כִּשְׁמֹעַ בְּקוֹל יְ־הֹוָה הִנֵּה שְׁמֹעַ מִזֶּבַח טוֹב לְהַקְשִׁיב מֵחֵלֶב אֵילִים: (שמואל א' ט"ו, כ"ב)

"But Samuel said: 'Does the LORD delight in burnt offerings and sacrifices as much as in obedience to the LORD's command? Surely, obedience is better than sacrifice, Compliance than the fat of rams'". (SAMUEL I 15:22)

לָמָּה־לִּי רֹב־זִבְחֵיכֶם יֹאמַר יְהֹוָה שָׂבַעְתִּי עֹלוֹת אֵילִים וְחֵלֶב מְרִיאִים וְדַם פָּרִים וּכְבָשִׂים וְעַתּוּדִים לֹא חָפָצְתִּי: (יְשַׁעְיָה א׳, י״א)

"'What need have I of all your sacrifices?' Says the LORD. 'I am sated with burnt offerings of rams and suet of fatlings, And I have no delight in blood of bulls, lambs and he-goats'". (ISAIAH 1, 11)

כִּי לֹא־דִבַּרְתִּי אֶת־אֲבוֹתֵיכֶם וְלֹא צִוִּיתִים בְּיוֹם הוֹצִיאִי אוֹתָם מֵאֶרֶץ מִצְרַיִם עַל־דִּבְרֵי עוֹלָה וָזָבַח: כִּי אִם־אֶת־הַדָּבָר הַזֶּה צִוִּיתִי אוֹתָם לֵאמֹר שִׁמְעוּ בְקוֹלִי וְהָיִיתִי לָכֶם לֵא־לֹהִים וְאַתֶּם תִּהְיוּ־לִי לְעָם״ (יִרְמְיָה ז׳, כ״ב-כ״ג)

"For when I freed your fathers from the land of Egypt, I did not speak with them or command them concerning burnt offerings or sacrifice. But this is what I commanded them: Do My bidding, that I may be your God and you may be My people". (JEREMIAH 7:22-23)

MAIMONIDES' Replies to Those Who Resist His Claims:

❚❚ They say: How can JEREMIAH say that GOD has not commanded us to offer sacrifices, seeing that so many commandments focus specifically on this?

The intent is, as I have explained to you, that GOD said: the first intention is for you to conceive Me, worship only Me and 'I will be your God and you shall be My people - 'וְהָיִיתִי לָכֶם לֵא־לֹהִים וְאַתֶּם תִּהְיוּ־לִי לְעָם (JEREMIAH 7:23). The laws concerning sacrifices and bringing them to THE TEMPLE were given only for the sake of your realization of this fundamental principle. It is for the sake of this principle that I transferred these modes of worship to My name, in order to erase the traces of idolatry, and the fundamental principle of My unity be established".

"One may say to you: Inasmuch as **GOD**'s first intention and will are that we should believe in this Law and that we should perform the actions prescribed by it, why did He not procure us the capacity to accept this intention and to act in accordance with it, instead of using a ruse with regard to us, declaring that He will procure us benefits if we obey Him, and will take vengeance on us if we disobey Him… What prevented Him from commanding us His real intention and causing us to have the ability to accept it?"

MAIMONIDES explains that although **GOD** changes the nature of things and people and performs miracles, He does not intervene with man's free choice:

❙❙Although all miracles change the nature of some individual beings, **GOD** does not change the nature of human individuals by means of miracles at all".

In other words, **GOD** does not restrict free will.

MAHARAM ALSHKAR defends MAIMONIDES' position, and opens his book "SEFER HAHASAGOT" with the following defense:

> ‏"קַנֹּא קִנֵּאתִי לִיסוֹד הַדָּת וְהָאֱמוּנָה / שֹׁרֶשׁ הַמַּדָּע וְהַתְּבוּנָה /
> עַמּוּד הַתּוֹרָה וְהַחָכְמָה הַתְּמִימָה / יַם הַדַּעַת וְהַמְזִמָּה /
> דֶּגֶל הַתְּעוּדָה / הַנּוֹדָע בְּיִשְׂרָאֵל וּבִיהוּדָה /
> הָרַב הַמֻּבְהָק, הֶחָסִיד הַגָּדוֹל /
> אוֹר הָעוֹלָם וּפִלְאוֹ / מוֹשָׁב הַיָּקָר וְשִׂיאוֹ /
> הוּא קְדוֹשׁ הָרַמְבַּ"ם זַ"ל / אֲשֶׁר שָׂמוּ אוֹתוֹ הַמּוֹרִים /
> מַטָּרָה לְחִצֵּי סִכְלוּתָם / וּלְתַעַר לְשׁוֹנָם וְדִמְיוֹנָם".

"I zealously defend the principle of religion and faith,

the root of knowledge and understanding,

the pillar of wisdom and perfect TORAH,

the sea of intellect and calculation,

the flagship of religion,

the esteemed Rabbi in Israel and Judea,

the eminent and great pious Rabbi,

who is a light unto the world and one of its wonders,

the precious and pious dignitary,

The holy MAIMONIDES, may he rest in peace,

whose name has become a target

for the shafts of their wicked ignoramuses,

and who has been subjected

to their razor-sharp tongues and imaginations".

MAHARAM ALSHKAR quotes the sages in VAYIKRA RABBAH, as an ancient source supporting MAIMONIDES' opinion about the purpose of animal sacrifice.

❝ The ultimate reason for the KORBANOT (sacrifices) was to abolish faulty philosophies held by the people leading them to foolishly sacrifice to idols and stars. Due to the difficulty of completely breaking a habit, GOD in His wisdom commanded us to no longer sacrifice to images devoid of substance and instead to sacrifice to His blessed name and commanded us to build Him a Temple. These are his general words in chapter 32 part 3. However, light opened my eyes to see that these are indeed the words of RABBI PINCHAS BEN YAIR in VAYIKRA RABBAH, who interprets the verse (VAYIKRA 17:7) **'And they shall no longer slaughter their sacrifices to the satyrs -** 'וְלֹא־יִזְבְּחוּ עוֹד אֶת־זִבְחֵיהֶם לַשְּׂעִירִם.

RABBI PINCHAS BEN YAIR says: "This is analogous to a King who had a son who ate scavenged and NON-KOSHER animals. The King pondered, what can be done to change this behavior? Because this behavior was ingrained in him, it seemed impossible. So the King said: *Let him eat at my table, and by eating my food he will no longer eat the defiled meat'* for it is written (VAYIKRA 17:5, 7), **'so that the children of Israel would bring their sacrifices which they offer... and they will no longer sacrifice to the demons -** לְמַעַן אֲשֶׁר יָבִיאוּ בְּנֵי יִשְׂרָאֵל אֶת־זִבְחֵיהֶם אֲשֶׁר הֵם זְבָחִים ... וְלֹא־יִזְבְּחוּ עוֹד אֶת־זִבְחֵיהֶם לַשְּׂעִירִם".

"The reason is that because the Israelites were eager to follow idolatry in Egypt and offered their sacrifices to demons, as it is written: (VAYIKRA 17:7) **'And they shall no more sacrifice their sacrifices unto the satyrs -** וְלֹא

יִזְבְּחוּ עוֹד אֶת־זִבְחֵיהֶם לַשְּׂעִירִם', which are demons, as it says: (DEVARIM 32) 'They sacrificed unto demons - יִזְבְּחוּ לַשֵּׁדִים'. They would offer these sacrifices at false Temples and then tragedies would befall them. Therefore **GOD** decided that they sacrifice to Him at all times in his tabernacle so that they gradually abandon idolatry and be saved".

(VAYIKRA RABBAH, chapter 22)

Now we will quote from a few of the Prophets and the later biblical books which admonish Israel for worshipping idols and sacrificing their sons to the MOLECH.

וַיִּזְבְּחוּ אֶת־בְּנֵיהֶם וְאֶת־בְּנוֹתֵיהֶם לַשֵּׁדִים: וַיִּשְׁפְּכוּ דָם נָקִי דַּם־בְּנֵיהֶם
וּבְנוֹתֵיהֶם אֲשֶׁר זִבְּחוּ לַעֲצַבֵּי כְנָעַן וַתֶּחֱנַף הָאָרֶץ בַּדָּמִים:

(תְּהִלִּים ק״ו, ל״ז-ל״ח)

"Their own sons and daughters they sacrificed to demons. They shed innocent blood, the blood of their sons and daughters, whom they sacrificed to the idols of Canaan; so the land was polluted with bloodguilt".

(PSALMS 106:37-38)

וּבָנוּ בָּמוֹת הַתֹּפֶת אֲשֶׁר בְּגֵיא בֶן־הִנֹּם לִשְׂרֹף אֶת־בְּנֵיהֶם וְאֶת־בְּנֹתֵיהֶם
בָּאֵשׁ אֲשֶׁר לֹא צִוִּיתִי וְלֹא עָלְתָה עַל־לִבִּי: (יִרְמִיָה ז׳, ל״א)

"And they have built the shrines of Topheth in the Valley of Ben-hinnom to burn their sons and daughters

in fire — which I never commanded, which never came
to My mind".

(JEREMIAH 7:31)

בַּמָּה אֲקַדֵּם יְהֹוָה אִכַּף לֵאלֹהֵי מָרוֹם הַאֲקַדְּמֶנּוּ בְעוֹלוֹת בַּעֲגָלִים
בְּנֵי שָׁנָה: הֲיִרְצֶה יְהֹוָה בְּאַלְפֵי אֵילִים בְּרִבְבוֹת נַחֲלֵי־שָׁמֶן הַאֶתֵּן
בְּכוֹרִי פִּשְׁעִי פְּרִי בִטְנִי חַטַּאת נַפְשִׁי: הִגִּיד לְךָ אָדָם מַה־טּוֹב וּמָה־
יְהֹוָה דּוֹרֵשׁ מִמְּךָ כִּי אִם־עֲשׂוֹת מִשְׁפָּט וְאַהֲבַת חֶסֶד וְהַצְנֵעַ לֶכֶת עִם־
אֱלֹהֶיךָ:
(מִיכָה ו׳, ו׳-ח׳)

"With what shall I approach the LORD, Do homage to
God on high? Shall I approach Him with burnt offerings,
With calves a year old? Would the LORD be pleased
with thousands of rams, With myriads of streams of
oil? Shall I give my first-born for my transgression,
The fruit of my body for my sins? He has told you, O
man, what is good, And what the LORD requires of
you: Only to do justice And to love goodness, And to
walk modestly with your God".

(MICHAH 6:6-8)

Also, this verse in Psalms is consistent with **MAIMONIDES'**
understanding:

זֶבַח וּמִנְחָה | לֹא־חָפַצְתָּ אָזְנַיִם כָּרִיתָ לִּי עוֹלָה וַחֲטָאָה לֹא שָׁאָלְתָּ:
(תְּהִלִּים מ׳, ז׳)

"You gave me to understand that You do not desire
sacrifice and meal offering; You do not ask for burnt
offering and sin offering".

(PSALMS 40:7)

In these words **KING DAVID** expresses **GOD**'s lack of desire for our sacrifices. **"You have made me ears -** אָזְנַיִם כָּרִיתָ לִּי" - You gave me ears to listen and understand that you did not ask for this.

RASHI comments on this verse and like MAIMONIDES he quotes JEREMIAH: **"'You desired neither sacrifice nor meal offering -** זֶבַח וּמִנְחָה | לֹא־חָפַצְתָּ'. When THE TORAH was given it was said (SHEMOT 19:5), 'Now, if you will listen to the voice of God... -** וְעַתָּה אִם־ שָׁמוֹעַ תִּשְׁמְעוּ בְּקֹלִי'** (and it does not mention sacrifices). Also, in JEREMIAH (7:22) He says, **'For neither did I speak with your forefathers nor did I command them to sacrifice ... -** ... כִּי לֹא־דִבַּרְתִּי אֶת־אֲבוֹתֵיכֶם וְלֹא צִוִּיתִים'**".

THE CHIDA (Rabbi Chayim Yosef David Azulai) states:

❝ Israel enthusiastically sacrificed to alien Gods. Because they were so accustomed to these practices, inhibiting them from sacrificing altogether was very difficult. Therefore, GOD commanded that they sacrifice to Him [...] as stated (VAYIKRA 17:5), **'So that they offer sacrifices which they offer in the fields -** לְמַעַן אֲשֶׁר יָבִיאוּ בְּנֵי יִשְׂרָאֵל אֶת־זִבְחֵיהֶם אֲשֶׁר הֵם זֹבְחִים עַל־פְּנֵי הַשָּׂדֶה'**, implying that since the people were already offering sacrifices to alien GODS, let them offer them to GOD instead, smoothly transitioning them away from the demons. These are the words of my father of blessed memory. However, I have seen in his expositions at the beginning of VAYIKRA where he discusses the words of RAMBAM and explains differently; it appears in THE HOLY ZOHAR and the MIDRASH RABBAH, stating explicitly and in a straightforward manner of the same thing as **THE RAMBAM** has said".

(PNEI DAVID, VAYIKRA, PARASHAT ACHAREI-MOT-KEDOSHIM)

THE RITVA (RABBI YOM TOV BEN AVRAHAM ASHVILI):

> ❚❚ Distancing them from worshipping alien **GODS**, which is inherently significant, is of major significance to the Guide to the Perplexed as he indicates in several places (PART 3, 29-30). Therefore, in his opinion, even **SHABBAT** is superseded by sacrificial offerings to **GOD** [because it is so important to distance us from idol worship] [...] Furthermore, after THE TORAH was given, **BALAAM** the heathen Prophet sacrificed a cow and ram which he learned from our nation".

(SEFER HAZIKARON – DEFENDING MOREH NEVUCHIM [BY RAMBAM] FTOM THE OBJECTIONS OF THE RAMBAN)

In **RAV ALBO's SEFER HA'IKARIM** we find that a Christian scholar asks him about sacrifices and these are his words:

> ❚❚ A Christian scholar queried me [...] THE TORAH deals with killing an animal, burning its meat and fat and throwing and sprinkling blood, all filthy acts [...]
>
> Regarding the description of the acts as 'filthy', i.e. incinerating the meat, fat and blood; if the command was given to transition the Jews from sacrificing to alien Gods as **RAMBAM** writes, it is quite understandable, because the purpose was to purify the hearts and halt the Jews from offering sacrifices to alien Gods.
>
> JEREMIAH said (7:22): 'For neither did I speak with

your forefathers nor did I command them on the day I brought them out of the land of Egypt concerning burnt offerings or sacrifices. But this I did command them, saying: Obey Me … - כִּי לֹא־דִבַּרְתִּי אֶת־אֲבוֹתֵיכֶם וְלֹא צִוִּיתִים בְּיוֹם הוֹצִיאִי אוֹתָם מֵאֶרֶץ מִצְרַיִם עַל־דִּבְרֵי עוֹלָה וָזָבַח: כִּי אִם־אֶת־הַדָּבָר הַזֶּה צִוִּיתִי אוֹתָם לֵאמֹר שִׁמְעוּ בְקוֹלִי". (Sefer Ha'Ikarim 43:25)

The Rambam's words have been criticized numerous times and most notably by Ramban. However, This criticism has already been rebuked with good taste and wisdom:

Rabbi Abarbanel's explanation of the Ramban's questions:

❞ The rational of sacrifices according to Rambam is that the worldwide custom practiced by all who worshipped their gods was to bring a variety of animals to The Temples where they served their idols by prostrating themselves and sacrificing to them […]

The Ramban wrote that Rambam's words are nonsense! As the Torah refers to sacrifices as 'fire-offering to God'. And when Noah exited the Ark he brought forth a sacrifice and the text says (Bereshit 8:21), 'God smelled the sweet smell - וַיָּרַח יְ־הוָה אֶת־רֵיחַ הַנִּיחֹחַ'. At that time there were no idol worshippers from which to distance oneself! 'And Abel himself brought forth a sacrifice from the firstborn of his flock and from the choicest and God listened to Abel - וְהֶבֶל הֵבִיא גַם־הוּא מִבְּכֹרוֹת צֹאנוֹ וּמֵחֶלְבֵהֶן וַיִּשַׁע יְ־הוָה אֶל־הֶבֶל' (Bereshit 4:4), but there were no idol worshippers yet in the world. And,

BALAAM said (BAMIDBAR 23:4), 'I have setup seven altars and brought forth a cow and ram upon the altar - אֶת־שִׁבְעַת הַמִּזְבְּחֹת עָרַכְתִּי וָאַעַל פָּר וָאַיִל בַּמִּזְבֵּחַ'. His intention was not to reject bad beliefs of which he was not commanded. Moreover, the terms **G**OD used to describe the sacrifices are (BAMIDBAR 28:2), 'My offering', 'My bread', 'My fires', 'My satisfying aroma' - אֶת־קָרְבָּנִי לַחְמִי לְאִשַּׁי רֵיחַ נִיחֹחִי - and heaven forbid that its purpose is to denounce idol worship and correct the mistaken.

The above is **R**AMBAN's argument against **R**AMBAM. [...] In the same article **R**AMBAN brings from the **S**IFRI and from the end of tractate **M**ENACHOT:

'**R**ABBI **S**HIMON BEN **A**ZAI says, come and see what is written in the Bible portion about sacrifices; the terms '**E**L' and '**E**LOHIM' are not used in this context, but rather the name **YHVH**\י־ה־ו־ה, which is the unified name representing **G**OD's mercy. This prevents one from arguing that sacrifices are for **G**OD to consume, as the verse states (PSALMS 50:13), 'Will I eat the flesh of bulls? - הַאוֹכַל בְּשַׂר אַבִּירִים'. I did not tell you to sacrifice to Me so that you can say, 'we will do His will'. You are not sacrificing because it is My will, it is rather because of your inner desire; as the verse states (VAYIKRA 22:29), 'According to your will you shall sacrifice - לִרְצֹנְכֶם תִּזְבָּחוּ'.

The **R**AMBAN cites the beginning of this quotation and leaves out its ending because it very much agrees with **R**AMBAM. And that which **R**ABBI **S**HIMON **B**EN **A**ZAI notes that with regard to the sacrifices only the name

YHVH\י״ה״ו״ה is employed, this is also consistent with RAMBAM – that the sacrifices were to distance the people from idol worship and bring them close to worshipping the true GOD. Thus no name other than YHVH\י״ה״ו״ה, the one unified name, is used in this context, as if to say, 'we are sacrificing to Him and not to alien Gods'.

Likewise, we find in the chapter entitled 'THE FORBIDDEN' (TMURAH, 28A):

'Thus, says TUVIA BEN MATANYAH in the name of RAV YOSHIYAHU: what does it mean (BAMIDBAR 28:2), 'You shall take care to offer to Me at the appointed time - תִּשְׁמְרוּ לְהַקְרִיב לִי בְּמוֹעֲדוֹ'? The implication is, sacrifice to 'Me - לִי' and NOT to another master. Who is the other master to whom they would sacrifice? To alien Gods!

All of these statements seem to be very consistent with RAMBAM's opinion regarding sacrifices. Moreover, note in another article in VAYIKRA RABBAH in ACHREI MOT, the section referring to one who sacrifices outside the camp:

RABBI PINCHAS says in the name of RAV LEVI, this is analogous to a prince who has become coarse and eats scavenged and non-KOSHER animals. Said the King: 'Let him always eat at this table and he will refine himself'. Similarly, Israel went with fervor after alien GODS and would offer forbidden sacrifices to the demons, and troubles and calamities befell them. Said The Blessed one be He: 'Let them offer sacrifices before Me in the Tent of Meeting and they will separate themselves from the alien GODS'. Accordingly, the law is, 'any man who slaughters outside'.

So this article clearly demonstrates their understanding of the sacrifices to be aligned with that of THE RAMBAM.

One cannot reasonably argue that this section of THE TORAH refers only to the peace offering because it mentions all of the sacrifices as the verse says (VAYIKRA 17:5):

לְמַעַן אֲשֶׁר יָבִיאוּ בְּנֵי יִשְׂרָאֵל אֶת־זִבְחֵיהֶם אֲשֶׁר הֵם זֹבְחִים עַל־פְּנֵי הַשָּׂדֶה וֶהֱבִיאֻם לַי־הֹוָה וְגוֹ'. וְלֹא־יִזְבְּחוּ עוֹד אֶת־זִבְחֵיהֶם לַשְּׂעִירִם אֲשֶׁר הֵם זֹנִים וְגוֹ'. וַאֲלֵהֶם תֹּאמַר אִישׁ אִישׁ מִבֵּית יִשְׂרָאֵל וּמִן־הַגֵּר אֲשֶׁר־יָגוּר בְּתוֹכָם אֲשֶׁר־יַעֲלֶה עֹלָה אוֹ־זָבַח: וְאֶל־פֶּתַח אֹהֶל מוֹעֵד לֹא יְבִיאֶנּוּ לַעֲשׂוֹת אֹתוֹ לַי־הֹוָה וְנִכְרַת הָאִישׁ הַהוּא מֵעַמָּיו.

'In order that the children of Israel should bring their offerings which they slaughter on the open field and bring them to the Lord...

And they shall no longer slaughter their sacrifices to the satyrs after which they stray...

And you should say to them: Any man of the House of Israel or of the strangers who will sojourn among them, who offers up a burnt offering or [any other] sacrifice, but does not bring it to the entrance of the Tent of Meeting to make it [a sacrifice] to the Lord, that man shall be cut off from his people'.

The command not to eat blood immediately follows this, as the verse states (VAYIKRA 17:10), 'Any man of the House of Israel... who eats any blood - וְאִישׁ אִישׁ מִבֵּית יִשְׂרָאֵל... אֲשֶׁר יֹאכַל כָּל־דָּם' - it is clear that this section of THE TORAH includes discussion not only of the blood but also of the burnt offering, the sacrificial offering and all sorts of sacrifices. Moreover, the verse does not say (VAYIKRA 17:7) 'And they shall no longer slaughter their sacrifices to the satyrs - וְלֹא־יִזְבְּחוּ עוֹד אֶת־זִבְחֵיהֶם לַשְּׂעִירִם' with regard to the blood alone, it is said in connection with the sacrifices. I wonder how it is that NACHMANIDES had THE TALMUD wide open before him - did he not see these words which agree with MAIMONIDES? **There is clear and strong support for MAIMONIDES opinion from THE TORAH, the Prophets, the scriptures and the words of our Rabbis in many places; MAIMONIDES' words are not nonsense; they are holy words!**

ADAM and his sons sacrificed as they considered themselves worshipping GOD by burning the fat and kidneys of a sacrificed animal upon the altar. It was as if they sacrificed their own innards; they considered the kidneys of the animal as their own kidney, in which thought originates; and the legs of the animal as representing their own hands and feet. And they threw the blood of the sacrifices instead of their own blood and acknowledged before GOD that it would be fitting to spill their own blood and burn their own body because of the sins they committed, if not for the kindness of GOD who was willing to receive from them the donation and the atonement of that sacrifice, in that it's blood and soul were in place of their own. NACHMANIDES has also mentioned this.

NOAH also sacrificed for the same reason as ADAM. In addition, he saw that the generation of the flood was undisciplined and worshipped alien Gods since the time of ENOSH, as the verse states (BERESHIT 6:11), 'The land became corrupt before God - וַתִּשָּׁחֵת הָאָרֶץ לִפְנֵי הָאֱ־לֹהִים'. Therefore, he brought sacrifices to spiritually grow and distance himself from idol worship. And it is true that BALAAM did not erect seven altars to distance himself from idol worship, but rather, as the reason is explained in BAMIDBAR RABBAH (CHAPTER 20):

'Why did he erect seven altars? To do as the seven most righteous individuals from the time of ADAM until MOSHE who built altars, sacrificed to GOD and were accepted'.

These are the great individuals who had their sacrifices received by GOD: ADAM, ABEL, NOAH, ABRAHAM, YITZCHAK, JACOB and MOSHE.

And regarding that which NACHMANIDES said about how sacrifices are described in THE TORAH (VAYIKRA 1:9): 'a fire and sweet smell to God - אִשֶּׁה רֵיחַ־נִיחוֹחַ לַי־הֹוָה' and (VAYIKRA 21:6) 'the bread of God - לֶחֶם אֱ־לֹהֵיהֶם', there is no doubt that MAIMONIDES would reply in accordance with his understanding and rationale that THE TORAH uses common terminology regarding one who sacrifices, as in the verse (VAYIKRA 17:7), 'And they shall no more sacrifice their sacrifices unto the satyrs - וְלֹא־יִזְבְּחוּ עוֹד אֶת־זִבְחֵיהֶם לַשְּׂעִירִם'. And do not question what it said that (BOOKS OF CHRONICLES 2, 29:6-7): 'Our forefathers acted improperly and did evil in the eyes of God ... and closed the great hall and extinguished the candles and did not offer the incense and the burnt offering to the God of Israel - כִּי־מָעֲלוּ אֲבֹתֵינוּ וְעָשׂוּ הָרַע בְּעֵינֵי יְ־הוָה ... גַּם סָגְרוּ דַּלְתוֹת הָאוּלָם וַיְכַבּוּ אֶת־הַנֵּרוֹת וּקְטֹרֶת לֹא הִקְטִירוּ וְעֹלָה לֹא־הֶעֱלוּ בַקֹּדֶשׁ לֵא־לֹהֵי יִשְׂרָאֵל'. His complaint was not that they did not bring the burnt offering for its own sake, but to say that in their rebellion and sins the kings of Yehuda were drawn to alien Gods; they closed the doors of The Temple, and canceled the worship, which is as if they threw off the yoke of Torah and Godly commandments.

In Midrash Shir Hashirim it says (Shir Hashirim 1:15), 'Behold, you are fair, my beloved - הִנָּךְ יָפָה רַעְיָתִי'; 'It is as if God said to Israel, 'you sustain Me' as the verse states (Bamidbar 28:2), 'My sacrifice, My bread - אֶת־קָרְבָּנִי לַחְמִי', but does God eat and drink? It comes to teach us that 'to My fire - לְאִשַּׁי' means that you are sacrificing for My fire. Why then does it say 'My bread - לַחְמִי'? To imply that even though you are sacrificing for fires, I consider it as if it were a human who sustains his father.

This article demonstrates that God has no physical wants or needs for sacrifices, and that the words (Bamidbar 28:2) 'My fire - לְאִשַּׁי' mean, as the friend of the King of the Khazars answered when he was asked about this, that the roaring fire and flames consumed the fully burnt sacrifice, but that even though you bring it to the fire, I consider it like a person who sustains their father.

And I am informing you of the opinion of Maimonides on this matter when he said that the sacrifices were brought based on the second intention, but he did not say that they will not be according to the first intention; this is the terminology of the Guide for the Perplexed that there are two intentions in sacrifices: The first intent is to have a human come close to their GOD and to subjugate themselves before Him, believe in His essence and unity and divine providence. This is the intent ADAM and NOAH had when they brought their sacrifice, and MAIMONIDES will not deny that it is found in the commandant for sacrifices. In fact, this was their original intention. However, for the human to be wholesome and achieve the true beliefs, MAIMONIDES saw that the first intention was mentioned far more in the prayers, true knowledge and other commandments directed toward this goal, and the intention in the sacrificing of fat and blood and the burning of the animal's body is to cling to GOD. Thus, MAIMONIDES said that GOD commanded the bringing of sacrifices to achieve cleaving to GOD and truly knowing Him because in those days all people were used to bringing sacrifices and completely breaking away from that which is customary is difficult. However, He commanded that we should do this to His name so that by doing so they would reach the original intent of achieving faith in GOD and distancing themselves from idolatry.

Hence, we have two intentions behind the sacrifices according to MAIMONIDES; the first, the only one which is in agreement with RAMBAN and the second. GOD intended both of them with this commandment and when you comprehend the truth of the matter, no doubts will remain with regard to **RAMBAN**'s questioning THE **RAMBAM**. This is what I have seen fit to suggest on this matter".

(ABARBANEL INTRODUCTION ON VAYIKRA)

THE HOLY ALSHEICH [RABBI MOSHE ALSHEICH]:

❝ There is a further proof to this, and it is […] 'that God commanded Moshe at Mount Sinai - אֲשֶׁר צִוָּה יְ־הֹוָה אֶת־מֹשֶׁה בְּהַר סִינַי' (VAYIKRA 7:38), the place of receiving THE TORAH from on high, and **there God did not command sacrifices**. When the children of Israel were commanded to sacrifice to **GOD** they were in the Sinai desert and not at Mount Sinai. **This was after the sin of the golden calf** and they were not at the mountain, they were in the desert. It was there that they were commanded to bring sacrifices to repair their sin. But this was not when they were at their height of sanctity when they stood at Mount Sinai. If so, we must ask which is greater: that which was stated at Sinai or that which came after? […] This is what the Prophet JEREMIAH said (JEREMIAH 7:22): **'For when I freed your fathers from the land of Egypt, I did not speak with them or command them concerning burnt offerings or sacrifice** - כִּי לֹא־דִבַּרְתִּי אֶת־אֲבוֹתֵיכֶם וְלֹא צִוִּיתִים בְּיוֹם הוֹצִיאִי אוֹתָם מֵאֶרֶץ מִצְרַיִם עַל־דִּבְרֵי עוֹלָה וָזָבַח". (ALSHEICH, VAYIKRA 7)

RABBI MEIR SIMCHA HAKOHEN from DVINSK:

❝ The intent is as follows: it is known that idol worship i.e. Pagan worship aimed to give pleasure and pay homage to the influential powers (according to their imagination) by dedicating their lives to them, sacrificing their sons and daughters, congregating, and scratching themselves with the purpose of amplifying the cruelty and vengefulness within the human soul, as the Prophet states (HOSHE'A 13:2), **'Those who sacrifice man might kiss calves -** זֹבְחֵי אָדָם **עֲגָלִים יִשָּׁקוּן'.** It was not until **GOD** enlightened the world with the light of His TORAH in which He commanded the commandments to Israel for their benefit and for the purpose of enabling them to complete their essence, not for His fulfillment! **'If you are righteous, what are you giving Him? -** אִם־צָדַקְתָּ מַה־תִּתֶּן־לוֹ' (JOB 35:7) [...] **GOD** has no use for animal sacrifice and does not desire the sacrifice, rather He wishes only for man to perform kindness and to walk in His ways. Therefore, **'it is for you that you shall slaughter it -** לִרְצֹנְכֶם תִּזְבָּחוּ' (VAYIKRA 19:5), i.e., when one should proclaim, 'it is my desire!' So take note, my sons, not to instruct acts of cruelty. **GOD** is merely asking you to **'Keep my commandments and perform them ... And do not desecrate my holy name -** וּשְׁמַרְתֶּם מִצְוֹתַי וַעֲשִׂיתֶם אֹתָם ... וְלֹא תְחַלְּלוּ אֶת־שֵׁם קָדְשִׁי' (VAYIKRA 22:31-32), for His good name proves that He established and sustains life in the worlds and wants them to endure, and does not want the destruction of his creations".

(MESHEKH CHOKHMAH, VAYIKRA, EMOR)

RABBI TZADOK HACOHEN from LUBLIN:

❞ The reasoning behind sacrifices was that the entity receiving the offering benefits from it. In Pagan worship, the specific idol supposedly derives energy and strength from the sacrifice, as a person does from food. And since they knew this regarding idol worship, their desire was to give the same to **GOD**. And upon this it says, **'You desire the work of your hands - לְמַעֲשֵׂה יָדֶיךָ תִכְסֹף'** (Job 14:15), as our Rabbis have said (MIDRASH TANCHUMA, TETZAVEH 2): **GOD** has allowed them to perform this act as though they were benefiting Him. It is only they who truly need this benefit gain from it, but **GOD** does not! Do not say, 'I will fulfill His will'... because as with all **MITZVOT**, they are according **'to your desire - לִרְצֹנְכֶם'** (VAYIKRA 19:5), and so is the sacrifice".   (TZIDKAT HATZADIK, PARAGRAPH 42)

RABBI YITZCHAK HEBENSTREIT:

❞ **REISH LAKISH** said: What is the meaning of that which is written (VAYIKRA 7:37): **'This is THE TORAH law of the burnt offering, of the meal offering... - זֹאת הַתּוֹרָה לָעֹלָה לַמִּנְחָה'?** This teaches that anyone who engages in TORAH study is considered as though he sacrificed a burnt offering, a meal offering, a sin offering and a guilt offering. **RAVA** raised an objection to this interpretation: This verse states: 'Of the burnt offering, of the meal offering'. If the interpretation of **REISH LAKISH** is correct, the verse should have written: 'Burnt offering and meal offering'. Rather, **RAVA** says that the correct interpretation of this verse is: Anyone who engages in TORAH study does not need to bring any of the offerings. **RABBI YITZCHAK** said: What is the meaning of that which is written (VAYIKRA 6:18): 'This is THE TORAH law of the sin offering - זֹאת תּוֹרַת הַחַטָּאת', and (VAYIKRA 7:1): 'This is THE TORAH law of the guilt offering - וְזֹאת תּוֹרַת הָאָשָׁם'? These verses teach that anyone who engages in studying the law of the sin offering is ascribed credit as though he sacrificed a sin offering. (MENACHOT 110)

This quotation cries out for explanation, as its entirety is difficult to comprehend; for according to **REISH LAKISH** one who studies TORAH needs never to bring a sacrifice. This is questionable because we can infer that if one studies TORAH, they are free from performing all MITZVOT and this cannot be, as there is a time for learning TORAH and a time for fulfilling MITZVOT. As the adage reads (PSALMS 119:126), 'A time to do for the Lord; they have made void Your Torah - עֵת לַעֲשׂוֹת לַי־הוָה הֵפֵרוּ תוֹרָתֶךָ'. So why are sacrifices an exception to the rule, since we have not found any other MITZVAH which one is exempt from fulfilling due to TORAH learning? From the words of **RABBI YITZCHAK** here, who says that all who learn THE TORAH of sin offering are considered as if they brought a sin offering, it seems that this would be applicable to all other MITZVOT as well, for instance, that all who study THE TORAH law of TZIZIT are considered as if they wrapped themselves in TZIZIT; and all who learn THE TORAH law of TEFILLIN are considered as if they put on TEFILLIN [and so on, with other MITZVOT too]. And a general rule is: 'study is not the primary goal; rather, action is'. And another adage states, 'It would have been better for one who learns but does not fulfill the MITZVOT to not have been born'. And according to the words said to Ben Azai, 'There is a type of scholar who expounds well but does not fulfill his own teachings'. Thus, REISH LAKISH's words are puzzling.

RABBI YITZCHAK says: The meal offering differs from other sacrifices in that the term 'an individual' ['nefesh'] is used with regard to it. The Holy One, Blessed be He, said: the poor bring a meal offering (as it is less expensive than an animal offering) and I will ascribe to them the credit as if they offered their soul ['NAFSHO'] before Me. (MENACHOT 104)

These words of RABBI YITZCHAK need deep explanation and analysis. We can ask: if one is poor, and brings the MINCHA since they cannot afford a large animal, does it follow that they gain an advantage over the wealthy who brought from the choicest animals? Let the poor at best be equal to the rich, as the adage goes, **'One who brings more and one who brings less... - are both accepted, just so they attune their hearts to GOD'** but certainly not better than the rich person's sacrifice. Furthermore, why should the sacrifice of the rich be lacking as it does not include the term 'soul' ('NEFESH')? And, did we not learn the opposite from CAIN and ABEL? And it states (BERESHIT 4:4), **'And the Lord turned to ABEL and to his offering - But to Cain and to his offering He** did not turn - ‏וַיִּשַׁע יְ־הֹוָה אֶל־הֶבֶל וְאֶל־מִנְחָתוֹ: וְאֶל־קַיִן וְאֶל־‏ ‏מִנְחָתוֹ לֹא שָׁעָה‏'. We see explicitly that GOD turned to ABEL who brought from the firstborn of his flock and the fattest, thus GOD turned to him and received his offering, but to CAIN who brought from the fruits of the ground He did not turn and did not receive his offering; how then does RABBI YITZCHAK state the opposite?

One must know well that God never desired for man to bring sacrifices, and never commanded them, and anyone who states that GOD wants sacrifices is mistaken. Although we find entire chapters in THE TORAH containing laws of sacrifice, it is because at that point in time it was necessary, and there are reasons for this. Know that the commandments for sacrifices are not like other commandments that were given forever, because the majority of the Prophets raised their voice like a SHOFAR against sacrifices, and even our great scholars, the Masters of THE TALMUD. For each and every MITZVAH they made fences and guardrails, yet they viewed the laws of sacrifice with indifference. Not only did they not add stringencies to them, they were lenient regarding them and looked at them with antipathy, as I will explain.

The majority of the Prophets raised their voices like a SHOFAR against sacrificing, and I will bring you quotations from their words, and you will clearly see that GOD does not want sacrifices.

❧ SAMUEL the Prophet said (SAMUEL I 15:22):

"הַחֵפֶץ לַי־הֹוָה בְּעֹלוֹת וּזְבָחִים כִּשְׁמֹעַ בְּקוֹל יְ־הֹוָה הִנֵּה שְׁמֹעַ מִזֶּבַח
טוֹב לְהַקְשִׁיב מֵחֵלֶב אֵילִים״.

"Does the LORD delight in burnt offerings and sacrifices
As much as in obedience to the LORD's command?
Surely, obedience is better than sacrifice, Compliance
than the fat of rams".

❧ ISAIAH said (ISAIAH 1:11):

"לָמָה־לִּי רֹב־זִבְחֵיכֶם יֹאמַר יְ־הֹוָה שָׂבַעְתִּי עֹלוֹת אֵילִים וְחֵלֶב מְרִיאִים
וְדַם פָּרִים וּכְבָשִׂים וְעַתּוּדִים לֹא חָפָצְתִּי״.

"'What need have I of all your sacrifices?' Says the
LORD. 'I am sated with burnt offerings of rams and
suet of fatlings, And I have no delight in blood of bulls,
lambs and he-goats'".

Furthermore he says (ISAIAH 66:3):

"שׁוֹחֵט הַשּׁוֹר מַכֵּה־אִישׁ זוֹבֵחַ הַשֶּׂה עֹרֵף כֶּלֶב ... גַּם־הֵמָּה בָּחֲרוּ
בְּדַרְכֵיהֶם וּבְשִׁקּוּצֵיהֶם נַפְשָׁם חָפֵצָה:״

"for those who slaughter oxen and slay humans, Who
sacrifice sheep and immolateb dogs ... Just as they
have chosen their ways And take pleasure in their
abominations".

❧ JEREMIAH said (JEREMIAH 6:20):

"... עֹלוֹתֵיכֶם לֹא לְרָצוֹן וְזִבְחֵיכֶם לֹא־עָרְבוּ לִי״.

" ... Your burnt offerings are not acceptable And your
sacrifices are not pleasing to Me".

and also (Jeremiah 7:22-23):

‫"כֹּה אָמַר יְ־הוָה צְבָאוֹת אֱ־לֹהֵי יִשְׂרָאֵל עֹלוֹתֵיכֶם סְפוּ עַל־זִבְחֵיכֶם‬
‫וְאִכְלוּ בָשָׂר: כִּי לֹא־דִבַּרְתִּי אֶת־אֲבוֹתֵיכֶם וְלֹא צִוִּיתִים בְּיוֹם הוֹצִיאִי‬
‫אוֹתָם מֵאֶרֶץ מִצְרָיִם עַל־דִּבְרֵי עוֹלָה וָזָבַח".‬

"Thus said the LORD of Hosts, the God of Israel: Add
your burnt offerings to your other sacrifices and eat the
meat. For when I freed your fathers from the land of
Egypt, I did not speak   with them or command them
concerning burnt offerings or sacrifice".

❧❧ HOSHE'A said (Hoshe'a 6:6):

‫"כִּי חֶסֶד חָפַצְתִּי וְלֹא־זָבַח וְדַעַת אֱ־לֹהִים מֵעֹלוֹת".‬

"For I desire goodness, not sacrifice; Obedience to God,
rather than burnt offerings".

❧❧ AMOS said (Amos 5:21-23):

‫"שָׂנֵאתִי מָאַסְתִּי חַגֵּיכֶם וְלֹא אָרִיחַ בְּעַצְּרֹתֵיכֶם: כִּי אִם־תַּעֲלוּ־לִי‬
‫עֹלוֹת וּמִנְחֹתֵיכֶם לֹא אֶרְצֶה וְשֶׁלֶם מְרִיאֵיכֶם לֹא אַבִּיט: הָסֵר מֵעָלַי‬
‫הֲמוֹן שִׁרֶיךָ וְזִמְרַת נְבָלֶיךָ לֹא אֶשְׁמָע".‬

"I loathe, I spurn your festivals, I am not appeased by
your solemn assemblies. If you offer Me burnt offerings
— or your meal offerings — I will not accept them; I
will pay no heed To your gifts of fatlings. Spare Me the
sound of your hymns, And let Me not hear the music of
your lutes".

❧❧ **MICHAH** said (MICHAH 6:6-7):

"בַּמָּה אֲקַדֵּם יְהוָה אִכַּף לֵא-לֹהֵי מָרוֹם הַאֲקַדְּמֶנּוּ בְעוֹלוֹת בַּעֲגָלִים בְּנֵי שָׁנָה: הֲיִרְצֶה יְהוָה בְּאַלְפֵי אֵילִים בְּרִבְבוֹת נַחֲלֵי-שָׁמֶן הַאֶתֵּן בְּכוֹרִי פִּשְׁעִי פְּרִי בִטְנִי חַטַּאת נַפְשִׁי".

"With what shall I approach the LORD, Do homage to God on high? Shall I approach Him with burnt offerings, With calves a year old? Would the LORD be pleased with thousands of rams, With myriads of streams of oil? Shall I give my first-born for my transgression, The fruit of my body for my sins?"

❧❧ **KING DAVID** said (PSALMS 40:7):

"זֶבַח וּמִנְחָה ׀ לֹא-חָפַצְתָּ אָזְנַיִם כָּרִיתָ לִּי עוֹלָה וַחֲטָאָה לֹא שָׁאָלְתָּ".

"You gave me to understand that you do not desire sacrifice and meal offering; You do not ask for burnt offering and sin offering".

And he says (Psalms 50:8, 13):

"לֹא עַל-זְבָחֶיךָ אוֹכִיחֶךָ וְעוֹלֹתֶיךָ לְנֶגְדִּי תָמִיד: ... הַאוֹכַל בְּשַׂר אַבִּירִים וְדַם עַתּוּדִים אֶשְׁתֶּה".

" I censure you not for your sacrifices, and your burnt offerings, made to Me daily; ... Do I eat the flesh of bulls, or drink the blood of he-goats?

Again, in Psalms (PSALMS 51:18) he says:

"כִּי ׀ לֹא-תַחְפֹּץ זֶבַח וְאֶתֵּנָה עוֹלָה לֹא תִרְצֶה".

"You do not want me to bring sacrifices; You do not desire burnt offerings".

✽ The wise KING SOLOMON states (PROVERBS 21:3):

"עֲשֹׂה צְדָקָה וּמִשְׁפָּט נִבְחָר לַי־הוָה מִזָּבַח".

"To do what is right and just Is more desired by the LORD than sacrifice".

Many more similar explicit verses can be found in our Holy books, but this sampling should suffice, now go and study the rest!

Our great scholars made boundaries and guardrails for every Mitzvah but with regard to sacrifices, they approached it with antipathy. Not only did they not make stringencies; they were lenient.

In addition to the above quotations, we find many more similar statements such as (MENACHOT 110):

"I did not say to you: Sacrifice offerings to me, so that you will say: I will do His will, i.e., fulfill His needs, and He will do my will. You are not sacrificing to fulfill My will, i.e., My needs, but you are sacrificing to fulfill your own will".

and RABBI YEHOSHUA BEN LEVI says (MAKKOT 10):

What is the meaning of that which is written (PSALMS 122:1): 'A song of the ascents to David: I rejoiced when they said to me, let us go to the house of God - שִׁיר הַמַּעֲלוֹת לְדָוִד שָׂמַחְתִּי בְּאֹמְרִים לִי בֵּית יְ־הוָה נֵלֵךְ'? DAVID said before the Holy One, blessed be He: Master of the Universe, I heard people who were saying in reference to me: When will this old man die, and SOLOMON his son will come and build THE TEMPLE and we will ascend there for the pilgrimage Festival? The Holy One, Blessed be He, said to him (Psalms 84:11): 'One day in your courtyard is better than one thousand - כִּי טוֹב־יוֹם בַּחֲצֵרֶיךָ מֵאָלֶף' meaning, one day during which you engage in the study of Torah before Me is preferable to one thousand burnt offerings that your son Solomon is destined to sacrifice before Me upon the altar (see Kings I 3:4).

And they have said: (Megillah 3)

"And the angel said to Joshua: 'During the afternoon you neglected the afternoon daily offering due to the impending battle, and now, at night, you have neglected Torah study, and I have come to rebuke you'. Joshua said to him: 'For which of these sins have you come?' And the angel answered (Joshua 5:14): 'I have come now - עַתָּה בָאתִי', indicating that neglecting Torah study is more severe than neglecting to sacrifice the daily offering. Joshua immediately rectifies this as the verses states (Joshua 8:9,13): 'And Joshua lodged that night in the midst of the valley - וַיֵּלֶךְ יְהוֹשֻׁעַ בַּלַּיְלָה הַהוּא ... בְּתוֹךְ הָעֵמֶק', and Rabbi Yochanan said: This teaches that he spent the night in the depths of Halacha. And Rav Shmuel said: Torah study is greater than sacrificing the daily offerings, as it is stated (Joshua 5:14): 'I have come now - עַתָּה בָאתִי'.

Thus, we must descend into the depths of the matter and comprehend, why is the command regarding sacrifices different from all other Mitzvot?

Sacrifices are unlike other Mitzvot in the Torah that were commanded for eternity, and it was never

GOD's desire for people to offer Him sacrifices. And THE TORAH commands sacrifices only because at that juncture in history it was necessary, for two reasons.

The first reason is that the fraudulent belief was widespread among the nations who believed living creatures were deities. There were those who worshipped cattle, there were those who worshipped sheep and the like, and animals were so grand and sanctified in their eyes that they sacrificed their children to their gods; a human was slaughtered for the animal! They even sacrificed to a picture or statue of an animal. The Egyptians believed in sheep as the verse states (BERESHIT 46) 'All shepherds were despised by the Egyptians - כִּי־תוֹעֲבַת מִצְרַיִם כָּל־רֹעֵה צֹאן'. Likewise, it says (SHEMOT 8) 'But Moshe said, it is improper to do that, for we will be sacrificing the deity of the Egyptians before their eyes, so will they not stone us? וַיֹּאמֶר מֹשֶׁה לֹא נָכוֹן לַעֲשׂוֹת כֵּן כִּי תוֹעֲבַת מִצְרַיִם נִזְבַּח לַי־הֹוָה אֱ־לֹהֵינוּ הֵן נִזְבַּח אֶת־תּוֹעֲבַת מִצְרַיִם לְעֵינֵיהֶם וְלֹא יִסְקְלֻנוּ'. Now when Israel resided amongst them they learned from the Egyptians' deeds and clung to their gods, as our Rabbis restate the Angels conversation with GOD, 'These are Idol worshippers and these are Idol worshippers', and GOD wanted to uproot from the world, and from Israel in particular, this fraudulent belief. Therefore, when Israel exited Egypt GOD commanded for them to bring the Paschal sacrifice (SHEMOT 12:3): 'Speak to the entire community of Israel, saying: On the tenth of this month, let each one take a lamb for each parental home, a lamb for each household - דַּבְּרוּ אֶל־כָּל־עֲדַת יִשְׂרָאֵל לֵאמֹר בֶּעָשֹׂר לַחֹדֶשׁ הַזֶּה וְיִקְחוּ לָהֶם אִישׁ שֶׂה לְבֵית־אָבֹת שֶׂה לַבָּיִת'.

And it is stated (SHEMOT 12:21), 'Draw forth or buy for yourselves sheep - מִשְׁכוּ וּקְחוּ לָכֶם צֹאן', and our Rabbis explain this to mean: draw yourselves away from Egyptian idol worship. As the adage goes (MIDRASH RABBAH, SHEMOT 16) 'Draw forth or buy for yourselves sheep - מִשְׁכוּ וּקְחוּ לָכֶם צֹאן' and likewise (PSALMS 97:7) 'All worshippers of graven images will be ashamed - יֵבֹשׁוּ ׀ כָּל־עֹבְדֵי פֶסֶל'. When GOD told MOSHE to slaughter the Paschal Lamb MOSHE said, 'GOD, how can I do this? You know that sheep are the GODs of the Egyptians?' For it says (SHEMOT 8:22), 'Will we sacrifice the deity of the Egyptians before their eyes, and they will not stone us? - הֵן נִזְבַּח אֶת־תּוֹעֲבַת מִצְרַיִם לְעֵינֵיהֶם וְלֹא יִסְקְלֻנוּ'. GOD replied, 'By your life, Israel is not leaving here until they slaughter the GOD of the Egyptians in front of them so that I may inform them that their GOD is nothing'. Look and see how strong the belief in sheep was: when MOSHE came down from Mount Sinai a few hours late (according to their calculations) Israel was corrupted and made a statue of a calf. Therefore, at that time it was necessary that the commandant of sacrifices demonstrate to the world in general and specifically to Israel that no GODly substance at all resides in those gods. GOD's name was thereby sanctified in the world by bringing the sacrifices, not because of the specific act, but because the moment in time necessitated it, and it was a special order given for that particular situation.

Accordingly, we can explain the words of our Rabbis, RAVA and RAV YITZCHAK we quoted above. The primary reason for sacrifices was only to show and prove to the world that animals are not GODS. And since the world had already come to this recognition and the contamination of the golden calf had left Israel, why then would we need to continue to spill blood? Thus, we do not really need sacrifices anymore because the idea of animals' GODliness had ceased to exist, and it is sufficient to acknowledge that there is nothing of substance in these idols, therefore anyone who simply learns THE TORAH laws of a sacrifice is ascribed as having actually sacrificed, since learning THE TORAH reveals one's true beliefs, and this is adequate. This is similar to the Article of Faith, 'I fully believe that animals are not GODS' and therefore one who learns the laws of sacrifices is likened to one who has actually sacrificed.

The second reason for the commandant of sacrifices is that at that time the idea had spread to the nations that their GODS desired human sacrifice, and there are many writings that establish human sacrifice as a very widespread practice in the world.

It is stated a few times in THE TORAH:

"וּמִזַּרְעֲךָ לֹא־תִתֵּן לְהַעֲבִיר לַמֹּלֶךְ" (וַיִּקְרָא י״ח, כ״א)

"You shall not hand over any of your children to be passed through [the worship of] MOLECH". (VAYIKRA 18:21)

And:

‏" ... גַּם אֶת־בְּנֵיהֶם וְאֶת־בְּנֹתֵיהֶם יִשְׂרְפוּ בָאֵשׁ לֵאלֹהֵיהֶם" (דְּבָרִים י"ב, ל"א)

" ... even their sons and their daughters do they burn in fire to their gods".

(DEVARIM 12:31)

And you will find in the Prophets many texts like this as in ISAIAH (Isaiah 57:5):

‏"הַנֵּחָמִים בָּאֵלִים תַּחַת כָּל־עֵץ רַעֲנָן שֹׁחֲטֵי הַיְלָדִים בַּנְּחָלִים תַּחַת סְעִפֵי הַסְּלָעִים".

"You who inflamec yourselves Among the terebinths, Under every verdant tree; Who slaughter children in the wadis, Amongd the clefts of the rocks".

And also (HOSHE'A 13):

‏"וְעַתָּה | יוֹסִפוּ לַחֲטֹא וַיַּעֲשׂוּ לָהֶם מַסֵּכָה מִכַּסְפָּם כִּתְבוּנָם עֲצַבִּים מַעֲשֵׂה חָרָשִׁים כֻּלֹּה לָהֶם הֵם אֹמְרִים זֹבְחֵי אָדָם עֲגָלִים יִשָּׁקוּן".

"And now they go on sinning; They have made them molten images, Idols, by their skill, from their silver, Wholly the work of craftsmen. Yet for these they appoint men to sacrifice; They are wont to kiss calves!"

Also (PSALMS 106:35, 37-38):

‏"וַיִּתְעָרְבוּ בַגּוֹיִם וַיִּלְמְדוּ מַעֲשֵׂיהֶם: וגו' וַיִּזְבְּחוּ אֶת־בְּנֵיהֶם וְאֶת־בְּנוֹתֵיהֶם לַשֵּׁדִים: וַיִּשְׁפְּכוּ דָם נָקִי דַּם־בְּנֵיהֶם וּבְנוֹתֵיהֶם אֲשֶׁר זִבְּחוּ לַעֲצַבֵּי כְנַעַן וַתֶּחֱנַף הָאָרֶץ בַּדָּמִים" (תְּהִלִּים ק"ו, ל"ה, ל"ז-ל"ח)

And They mingled with the nations and learned their ways ... Their own sons and daughters they sacrificed to demons. They shed innocent blood, the blood of their sons and daughters, whom they sacrificed to the idols of Canaan; so the land was polluted with bloodguilt".

YIFTACH THE GILADI sacrificed his only daughter (JUDGES 11).

And also:

'So he [Meisha the king of Moab] took his first-born son, who was to succeed him as king, and offered him up on the wall as a burnt offering - וַיִּקַּח אֶת־בְּנוֹ הַבְּכוֹר אֲשֶׁר־יִמְלֹךְ תַּחְתָּיו וַיַּעֲלֵהוּ עֹלָה' (KINGS 2, 3:27).

We find in our Rabbis' writings (SANHEDRIN 39) that there is an opinion that MEISHA intended to act for the sake of Heaven; when MEISHA, the king of MOAB, placed his son on the altar he said, 'Creator of the world, ABRAHAM placed his son on the altar and did not slaughter him, but I will indeed slaughter my son and raise him in a completely burnt offering'. But GOD wanted to prevent human sacrifice, because human sacrifice even for the sake of Heaven is strictly forbidden as is written:

"כִּי כָל־תּוֹעֲבַת יְהֹוָה אֲשֶׁר שָׂנֵא עָשׂוּ לֵאלֹהֵיהֶם" (דְּבָרִים י"ב, ל"א)

"Because whatever is abominated by God, what He hates, they have done for their gods". (DEVARIM 12:31)

As brought in (TA'ANIT, 1ST CHAPTER):

"אֲשֶׁר לֹא־צִוִּיתִי וְלֹא דִבַּרְתִּי וְלֹא עָלְתָה עַל־לִבִּי" (יִרְמִיָה י"ט, ה')

"Which I never commanded, never decreed, and which never came to My mind". (Jeremiah 19:5)

'**Which I never commanded**' refers to the sacrificing of Meisha the King of Moab's son. As the text reads (Kings 2, 3:27):

"וַיִּקַּח אֶת־בְּנוֹ הַבְּכוֹר אֲשֶׁר־יִמְלֹךְ תַּחְתָּיו וַיַּעֲלֵהוּ עֹלָה עַל־הַחֹמָה וַיְהִי קֶצֶף־גָּדוֹל עַל־יִשְׂרָאֵל וַיִּסְעוּ מֵעָלָיו וַיָּשֻׁבוּ לָאָרֶץ" (מלכים ב׳ ג׳, כ״ז)

"So he took his first-born son, who was to succeed him as king, and offered him up on the wall as a burnt offering. A great wrath came upon Israel, so they withdrew from him and went back to [their own] land".

'**never decreed**' refers to the daughter of Yiftach the Giladi.

'**which never came to My mind**' refers to Yitzchak, the son of Abraham. Thus, when the Creator saw the cruel tendencies which arose from the fraudulent beliefs that spread wildly like locusts – people passed young children to Molech and those precious in His eyes were burnt to dust and became repugnant incense, they sacrificed suckling babies with their mother's milk still upon their lips. This one brings his only daughter as an offering and that one slaughters his firstborn son upon the wall. God therefore gave the law to sacrifice cattle and sheep instead of human sacrifice, because at that time it was necessary, because it was better to lose an animal than a human. And this is the way to understand The Binding of Yitzchak: God showed the world, through Abraham Our Father, the taking of an animal instead of a human.

"וַיִּקַּח אֶת־הָאַיִל וַיַּעֲלֵהוּ לְעֹלָה תַּחַת בְּנוֹ" (בְּרֵאשִׁית כ"ב, י"ג).

"And [he] took the ram and sacrificed it as a burnt-offering instead of his son".　(BERESHIT 22:13)

It was never GOD's intent for ABRAHAM to sacrifice YITZCHAK as an OLAH, nor to sacrifice animals, because GOD does not want the spilling of innocent blood.

However, it was impossible to entirely prevent sacrifices at that juncture since at the time people believed that the Creator needs to eat, and assumed they would satiate His hunger with the offering.

They were far from understanding that GOD does not desire sacrifices, therefore the first step in this education was to take an animal instead of a human, the living instead of a speaking (human), as is written (BERESHIT RABBAH 56): ABRAHAM OUR FATHER was shocked by GOD's quizzical words: "You first said (BERESHIT 21:12), 'for [only] through Yitzchak will seed be considered yours - כִּי בְיִצְחָק יִקָּרֵא לְךָ זָרַע'; then seeming to contradict this, You said (BERESHIT 22:2), 'Please Take your son - קַח־נָא אֶת־בִּנְךָ'. GOD replied: I did not say 'slaughter' him, I said in loving terms, 'raise him up - וְהַעֲלֵהוּ'.

'It was never my intent - וְלֹא עָלְתָה עַל־לִבִּי' (JEREMIAH 19) that you slaughter YITZCHAK'. And it is true that ABRAHAM could have brought a flour offering instead of his son, necessitating no spillage of blood. He did not bring a flour offering instead of the ram for two reasons:

1. ABRAHAM OUR FATHER was unaware of such a thing

as a flour offering, as is stated specifically (MIDRASHH RABBAH, VAYIKRA 3): **RABBI SHIMON BAR YOCHAI** says, 'GOD showed ABRAHAM all of the atonements other than 1/10 of an EIFAH'.

2. It was too early in human development for the concept that a flour offering could replace a human sacrifice. This understanding was distant at that time because to their way of thinking a sacrifice without spilt blood was insufficient as they believed a sacrifice had to be one soul in place of another; one's blood replaced with another's; whereas a flour offering involves no soul and no blood. And they specifically knew that CAIN brought fruit of the land and GOD did not turn to his offering, therefore with righteousness he was sacrificed and slaughtered a Ram.

Now those times with their strong belief in human sacrifice had passed, so why were there still sacrifices? We understand they originally came to replace human sacrifice; however, now that human sacrifice was no longer practiced why was the spilling of blood continued? This could be considered unnecessarily spilling blood thus violating the law not to murder. And if we cannot entirely do away with sacrifices, then sacrifices of '**flour mixed with oil** - סֹלֶת בְּלוּלָה בַשֶּׁמֶן' (VAYIKRA 2:5) could be brought without the need for spilling blood.

Therefore, **RABBI YITZCHAK** is correct when he asks, 'How does the MINCHA sacrifice differ from other sacrifices? In that the term 'soul' is associated with it'.

GOD said, 'What is the way of a poor person? To bring a MINCHA! I ascribe to them as if they brought their own soul before me'. The intent is that GOD sees greater value in the MINCHA comprised of flour than in any other sacrifice, because no spilling of blood is involved, and even though there is no soul given to GOD it is considered as if one sacrificed their soul to GOD.

One may certainly ask: from CAIN and ABEL we learn the opposite:

'... וַיִּשַׁע יְ־הֹוָה אֶל־הֶבֶל וְאֶל־מִנְחָתוֹ: וְאֶל־קַיִן וְאֶל־מִנְחָתוֹ לֹא שָׁעָה

(בְּרֵאשִׁית ד', ד'־ה')

'...

" ... Adonay paid regard to Hevel and to his offering. But to Kayin and his offering He paid no regard..."

(BERESHIT 4:4-5).

We explicitly see that GOD turned His face to ABEL's offering that was brought 'From the firstborn and fattest of his flock - מִבְּכֹרוֹת צֹאנוֹ וּמֵחֶלְבֵהֶן' (BERESHIT 4:4), but to CAIN who brought forth 'From the fruit of the ground - מִפְּרִי הָאֲדָמָה' (BERESHIT 4:3), GOD did not turn His face and did not accept his offering.

This question has already been asked in the SEFER HA'IKARIM (RABBI YOSEF ALBO) (ARTICLE 3, CHAPTER 15). CAIN killed ABEL for the following reason: CAIN believed that ABEL should be killed because he brought from the firstborn of his flock i.e. spilled the blood of a living creature, therefore CAIN spilled his blood, 'soul for a soul - נֶפֶשׁ תַּחַת נֶפֶשׁ' (SHEMOT 21:23).

The reason GOD did not turn His face to CAIN's

offering and that he received further punishment for killing **ABEL** is that **CAIN** himself did not walk the golden path, since he equated the value of an animal to that of a human. He felt a human was no greater than an animal - **GOD** therefore did not turn His face to **CAIN**'s offering. The truth that indeed is we do not have permission to spill blood of an animal, yet we are not supposed to equate an animal with a human. Because even though we do not have permission to slaughter, eat or to cause them pain, we do however have permission to use them as 'an animal was created to plough'.

From all the above we see that **GOD**'s desire is not to have us bring sacrifices, and that THE TORAH commands to bring sacrifices because it was necessary at that time, as we have explained. Thus, 'TORAH commandments' and 'The Creator's will' are not always the same, and so it is with sacrifices. This idea is explicitly expressed in our Rabbis' words (JERUSALEM TALMUD, MAKKOT 2:6):

'**Wisdom** was asked, how should a sinner be punished? It answered: "Misfortune pursues sinners - חַטָּאִים תְּרַדֵּף רָעָה" (Proverbs 13:21).

Prophecy was asked, how should a sinner be punished? It answered: "The sinful soul, [only she] shall die - הַנֶּפֶשׁ הַחֹטֵאת הִיא תָמוּת" (Ezekiel 18:4).

GOD was asked: what should a sinner's punishment be? He responded: "let them repent".

We see then that the "TORAH commandment" and "GOD's desire" with regard to sacrifices are not identical, for THE TORAH says, 'bring a sacrifice' and GOD says, 'let them repent'. The reason is as I explained that at the time it was necessary even though it was not the Creator's desire".

(RABBI YITZCHAK HEBENSTREIT: BOOK KIVROTH HATTA'AVAH)

RABBI SAMSON RAPHAEL HIRSCH:

❞ Wherever sacrifices are mentioned, GOD's name is written **YHWH** and not Elokim. Our Rabbis explain the reason for this is (SEE RABBI YOSSI'S WORDS AT SIFRA [HALAKHIC MIDRASH TO THE BOOK OF LEVITICUS], PARASHAT VAYIKRA, PARASHA 2:5) 'So as not to present an opening for the heretic to deny' i.e., to eradicate any hint of the similarity to the sacrifices of idol worship".

(BERESHIT 8)

RABBI AVRAHAM YITZCHAK KOOK:

❞ Since the human will cannot be perfected through this desire (to offer animal sacrifice), surely the high court will possess the power to interchange plant offerings in place of animal sacrifice. This is why the final document says (MALACHI 3:4): **'Then the offerings of Judah and Jerusalem shall be pleasing to the LORD as in the days of yore and in the years of old** - וְעָרְבָה לַי־הֹוָה מִנְחַת יְהוּדָה וִירוּשָׁלָם'. Take note, it says 'offering' and not 'burnt offering'. As our sages say: 'All of the sacrifices will be abolished except for the TODAH (thanks) offering, because it is mostly a bread offering, and that will not be abolished".

(LENEVUCHE HADOR, CHAPTER 10)

Rabbi Chayim Hirschinzon:

> ❝ It is obvious that in these enlightened times there is no thought of pleasing God 'With thousands of rivers of oil - בְּרִבְבוֹת נַחֲלֵי־שָׁמֶן' (Micha 6:7) […] one's heart does not want to believe that in the time to come when 'The world is filled with the knowledge of God - כִּי־מָלְאָה הָאָרֶץ דֵּעָה אֶת־יְ־הֹוָה' (Isaiah 11:9), the same idea of sacrifices held by the simple people when The Temple stood would still persist […] but it was not proper for Ezekiel to speak to the nation in his day about end times in terms they could comprehend". (Responsa Malki BaKodesh, part 1, section 10)

In a letter he sent to **Rabbi Avraham Yitzchak Kook**, **Rav Chayim Hirschinzon** writes,

> ❝ Knowledge and understanding do not revert to the past - for one culture to consider an unrefined concept to be refined". (Responsa Malki BaKodesh, part 4, letters)

❧ Summary: ❧

The commandment to offer sacrifices was given as a transitional step to breaking free from idol worship. At that time, there was no worship without sacrifice. The purpose of sacrifices was to distance the nation of Israel from worshipping alien Gods.

THE CUSTOM OF KAPAROT

Regarding the custom of KAPAROT, RABBI YOSEF KARO writes: **"This custom should be prevented!"** (SHULCHAN ARUCH, ORACH CHAYIM, SECTION 605). In the first copy of the SHULCHAN ARUCH ORACH CHAYIM, the caption of chapter 605 reads: **"The custom of KAPAROT on EREV YOM KIPPUR is a foolish custom"**. In later copies, they removed the words **"is a foolish custom"**.

Also the **RASHBA** [RABBI SHLOMO IBN ADERET] was against this custom:

> Even though I have heard from very decent people in ASHKENAZ who sit with us in the study hall that all of the Rabbis of their land do this on the eve of YOM KIPPUR and slaughter the goose or chicken [...] still I have disallowed this custom in our city". (RESPONSA HaRASHBA PART 1, SIMAN 395).

THE RAMBAN (SEE BEIT YOSEF, ORACH CHAYIM, SIMAN 605) and **RAMBAM** do not even mention the custom and therefore it was not done in Yemen.

Rabbi Chayim David HaLevi, the composer of the Kitzur Shulchan Aruch Mekor Chayim:

> ❚❚Why do we have to needlessly act cruelly to animals specifically on the eve of this holy day? And then to slaughter them with no mercy, at the very moment that we stand and ask for mercy for ourselves from the living God?"
>
> (Responsa Aseh Lecha Rav, part 3, 20)

The Rashbam [Rabbi Shmuel Ben Meir] is known as the literalist exegete, even when others interpreted the text differently and derived laws from it. His understanding of:

> ❚❚'To send (the goat) it off to the wilderness for Azazel - 'לְשַׁלַּח אֹתוֹ לַעֲזָאזֵל הַמִּדְבָּרָה is literal: this means to send the goat alive to the other goats in the desert. This is similar to the bird of the Leper: 'He shall then send away the live bird into the open field - וְשִׁלַּח אֶת־הַצִּפֹּר הַחַיָּה עַל־פְּנֵי הַשָּׂדֶה' (Vayikra 14:7) to purify the leper from his impurity. Here too, to purify Israel from their iniquities, the goat is sent to the desert where animals graze".
>
> (Rashbam on Vayikra 16:10)

This means that atonement derives specifically from the freeing of the live goat to wander amongst other goats, and not from killing it on a cliff.

Rabbi Yehudah Asad:

> ❚❚Slaughter needs to be explained as with each act of slaughter there is undue pain caused to an animal.

THE TORAH only permits one to **slaughter and eat** on condition that there is no cruelty in the act of slaughtering. However, on the Day of Judgment when we all seek mercy all day long, as it is written (Psalms 145:9), **'God is merciful to all of his creations** - וְרַחֲמָיו עַל־כָּל־מַעֲשָׂיו', it is fitting for us not to act cruelly and slaughter living creatures". (RESPONSA YEHUDAH YA'ALE, RABBI YEHUDAH ASAD,

PART 1, ORACH CHAYIM, SIMAN 164)

(RESPONSA HARABAZ, PART 1, ORACH CHAYIM, YOREH DE'AH, SIMAN 115)

THE RAMBAN [RABBI MOSHE BEN NACHMAN]:

❝ The reason to prevent this behavior is to **teach us mercy,** so we should not become cruel. Because cruelty can spread in one's soul, as is known with butchers who slaughter large oxen and donkeys; amongst these people are those who spill human blood as well and are very cruel. Because of this they said (KIDDUSHIN 82a): **'Even the best butcher is a partner with** AMALEK'". (RAMBAN, DEVARIM, 22)

RABBI NACHMAN OF BRESLOV:

❝ Rabbi Shimon wanted to teach himself SHECHITA (ritual slaughter) and asked the Rabbi. Our holy Rabbi advised him to learn to be a doctor instead. **RABBI SHIMON** said, **'Do you want me to become a murderer?'** The Rabbi responded, 'And isn't it murder when they take the chicken, who is a reincarnation of an old man, and grab him by the beard and slaughter him?' It was then that he decided not to learn to become a **SHOCHET** (slaughterer)". (KOCHVEY OHR [=STARS OF LIGHT],

BY RABBI ABRAHAM CHAZAN, SON OF REB NACHMAN TULCHYNER, SIMAN 65)

RABBI SAMSON RAPHAEL HIRSCH:

❚❚ Therefore, you parents and teachers, into whose hands has been placed the spirit of the youth and their education, watch over them closely in this matter and teach them to honor and recognize living creatures, small and large, as independent beings, for they too are God's creations. So that they know animals have feelings as they do, and feel pleasure and pain. And do not forget that even a youth with a noble heart who looks with delight at an injured locust twisting in anguish, or an injured creature on the precipice between life and death, seeing this often will turn their heart into stone. As a result, they will not sense or feel when seeing something bad happen to their friend, a person like themselves, and they will pay no attention to the intensity of their pain". (HOREB, 5:2)

YALKUT SHIMONI:

❚❚ Happy are the righteous ones whose animal is as beloved to them as their own body. As we find with **JACOB** who said to **YOSEF** (BERESHIT 37:14), 'Go now and see your brothers' welfare and the welfare of the flocks - לֶךְ־ נָא רְאֵה אֶת־שְׁלוֹם אַחֶיךָ וְאֶת־שְׁלוֹם הַצֹּאן' thereby applying the adage (Proverbs 12:10): 'the righteous know the soul of their animal - יוֹדֵעַ צַדִּיק נֶפֶשׁ בְּהֶמְתּוֹ'". (Yalkut Shimoni, Chukat) ❧

THE **PURPOSE** OF ANIMALS

I have found that there is a major gap between many peoples' views and the words we hear from our sages regarding the purpose of animals. I have heard false explanations of this many times. Therefore, I have collected some of the words of our first Geonim and **ACHRONIM** regarding the purpose of animals.

It should be pointed out that a few decisors understand the issue of TZA'AR BA'ALEI CHAYIM based solely on "a theory of belief" that animals were created only to serve man. However, many decisors – from the **"GREAT EAGLE" MAIMONIDES** to the great men of the last generation, amongst them **RABBI ELIYAHU KLETZKIN**, Head of the court in Lublin, object to this idea and explain that animals have been created for the purpose of their own existence.

The core of the assumption that animals were created to serve man is solely "a theory of belief". With regard to belief and knowledge, which constitute a basis for a theory of belief, MAIMONIDES comments in three places in his commentary on THE MISHNAH:

> ❚❚ when there is a difference of opinion between the sages on a theory of belief, which has no practical ramifications, we do not rule according to this one or the other".　(MAIMONIDES, COMMENTARY ON THE MISHNA, SOTAH 3:5)

> ❚❚ We have already mentioned numerous times that with regard to a difference of opinion between the sages which is not relevant to an act but to theory alone, there is no place to decide according to either of them".
>
> (MAIMONIDES, COMMENTARY ON THE MISHNA, SANHEDRIN 10:3)

> ❚❚ We have already explained that regarding all theories which do not relate to an actual deed on which the sages differ, we do not decide according to an individual party".　(MAIMONIDES, COMMENTARY ON THE MISHNA, SHEBU'OTH 1:4)

Therefore, when a scholar bases their decision solely on a theory of belief, their decision is weak and is clearly not binding; and when numerous decisors oppose them, their opinion is weakened even more. This is ever more so when we are dealing with a TORAH commandment.

Moreover, there is a general rule: "**when in doubt over a TORAH law, we follow the stricter opinion**". How then can we rely upon a theory of belief? Certainly, we cannot relate lightly to the commandment of

Tza'ar Ba'alei Chayim which is integrally related with mercy and based upon it one may experience consequences in their own life; good or bad; as our sages say in THE TALMUD, "one who is merciful toward the living, heaven acts mercifully toward them; but those who do not, heaven does not act mercifully toward them" (SHABBAT 151B).

"AND RULE OVER

THE FISH OF THE SEA AND OVER THE FOWL OF THE SKY AND OVER ALL THE BEASTS"

The first argument heard from people is the quote from the book of BERESHIT, **"And rule over the fish of the sea and over the fowl of the sky and over all the beasts -** "וּרְדוּ בִּדְגַת הַיָּם וּבְעוֹף הַשָּׁמַיִם וּבְכָל־חַיָּה" (BERESHIT 1:28). This quotation is puzzling, because the text specifies that man's nourishment is solely derived from vegetation and that at the outset eating meat was forbidden. How then could animals' purpose be for consumption if meat was forbidden at the beginning of creation?

Our scholars have asked this question, and they answer: the text is not granting permission to consume the animals; rather, it speaks of permitting their use for work purposes, as in the chapter entitled "FOUR TYPES OF THE DEATH" (Sanhedrin 59b) Our Rabbis explained, "GOD did not grant ADAM permission to eat animals but He did allow him rule over them so that they would obey him".

The GEMARA raises an objection to the assertion that eating meat was prohibited to ADAM, from the verse (BERESHIT 1:28): '**And rule over the fish of the sea and over the fowl of the air, and over every living thing that creeps upon the land** - וּרְדוּ בִּדְגַת הַיָּם וּבְעוֹף הַשָּׁמַיִם וּבְכָל־חַיָּה הָרֹמֶשֶׂת עַל־הָאָרֶץ'. What, is it not stated with regard to consumption, i.e., doesn't this verse mean that people may eat the meat of animals? The GEMARA answers: No, the verse is referring to using animals for labor. The GEMARA asks: But are fish capable of performing labor? Yes. (SANHEDRIN 59b)

RABBI ELIYAHU MIZRACHI:

❚❚ '**And rule over the fish of the sea** - וּרְדוּ בִּדְגַת הַיָּם' - you subjugate them but they do not subjugate you, however man is only permitted to eat vegetation and fruit from trees and is not to kill any being to eat its flesh. The verse (BERESHIT 1:28), '**And rule over the fish of the sea and over the fowl of the sky** - וּרְדוּ בִּדְגַת הַיָּם וּבְעוֹף הַשָּׁמַיִם', does not refer to permission to eat them, but rather to use them to perform work as stated in the chapter "FOUR TYPES OF THE DEATH" (SANHEDRIN 59b). And as for the fish of the sea and the birds in the sky, both which cannot perform work, it is already addressed in the **GEMARA**: In accordance with the statement of Rechava who asked the following question: If one drove a wagon to which a goat and a shibbuta fish were harnessed together, what is the **HALACHA**? And as **RABBA BAR RAV HUNA** raises a dilemma: If one threshed with geese and chickens, what is the **HALACHA**? **RASHI** explains: tie a wagon to a fish in the sea and a goat on the land and the two will pull it. And where is says: Angels were roasting meat for **ADAM**; we establish that this refers to meat that descended from heaven".

(HARE'EM, BERESHIT, CHAPTER 1)

RABBI SHABBETHAI BEN JOSEPH BASS:

❙❙'And rule over the fish of the sea and over the fowl - וּרְדוּ בִּדְגַת הַיָּם וּבְעוֹף' comes not to permit their consumption but to use them for labor.

(SIFTEI CHACHAMIM, BERESHIT, CHAPTER 1)

RABBI HEZEKIAH BEN MANOAH:

❙❙That which is written, 'and rule over the fish - וּרְדוּ בִּדְגַת הַיָּם' refers to using animals for labor [...] as is written in THE TALMUD (chapter "Four types of the death" - SANHEDRIN 59b)".

(CHIZKUNI, BERESHIT, CHAPTER 1)

RABBI ISAAC BEN JUDAH ABARBANEL:

❙❙'And rule over the fish of the sea - וּרְדוּ בִּדְגַת הַיָּם'.

RABBI NISSIM wrote: since it says 'fish of the sea - בִּדְגַת הַיָּם' one may suppose this verse permits man to consume them as it says: 'with all of their desire they may eat meat'. It is for this reason that **GOD** had to say, even though you may rule over them, you may not consume them".

(ABARBANEL BERESHIT, CHAPTER 1)

THE HOLY ALSHEICH [Rabbi Moshe Alsheich]:

❚❚ After the verse that states (BERESHIT 1:28) **'And rule over the fish of the sea - וּרְדוּ בִּדְגַת הַיָּם'** it says (BERESHIT 1:29), **'God says, I have given you all of the grass of the field - וַיֹּאמֶר אֱ-לֹהִים הִנֵּה נָתַתִּי לָכֶם אֶת־כָּל־עֵשֶׂב'**. These words show that eating the flesh of an animal was forbidden".

(ALSHEICH - BERESHIT CHAPTER 1)

RABBI BARUCH EPSTEIN:

❚❚ Even though it is written **'And rule over the fish of the sea and over the fowl of the sky and over all the beasts - וּרְדוּ בִּדְגַת הַיָּם וּבְעוֹף הַשָּׁמַיִם וּבְכָל־חַיָּה הָרֹמֶשֶׂת'** - this refers to using them for work" (SANHEDRIN 59b).

(TORAH TEMIMAH, BERESHIT CHAPTER 1)

RABBI MEIR HALEVI ABULAFIA:

❚❚ For what purpose was **ADAM** given dominion over animals? It was not for consumption, but they were uncertain about labor and inquired about the birds' ability to work. THE TALMUD answers: 'Yes, birds can work!'"

(YAD RAMAH - SANHEDRIN 59B)

RABBI YEHUDAH HACHASSID:

❙❙With regard to **BALAAM** the Angel asks (BAMIDBAR 22:32),
'Why did you strike your donkey? - עַל־מָה הִכִּיתָ אֶת־
אֲתֹנְךָ'. And because **BALAAM** said (BAMIDBAR 22:29): 'Would
that I had a sword in my hand, I would kill you now
- לוּ יֶשׁ־חֶרֶב בְּיָדִי כִּי עַתָּה הֲרַגְתִּיךְ', therefore **BALAAM** was
ultimately killed by the sword.

We have been warned; the **NOACHIDES** were not given
dominion over animals, whereas **ADAM**, while not granted
permission to eat meat, was granted dominion over them;
but **NOACHIDES** who were permitted to consume meat
were not granted dominion [...] this clearly indicates
that **as long as you are merciful, GOD will be merciful to
you**". (SEFER CHASIDIM, SIMAN 666)

RABBI ISRAEL BEN BENJAMIN OF BEŁŻEC:

❙❙That which it states, '**And rule over the fish of the sea
- וּרְדוּ בִּדְגַת הַיָּם**' specifically refers to the first man, who
was not granted permission to eat meat but was given
dominion. However, **NOACHIDES** who were allowed to
eat meat were not given dominion, therefore **BALAAM** was
punished". (BOOK "YALKUT CHADASH",

CHAPTER: "ADAM AND THE GENERATIONS UNTIL NOACH", SECTION 85)

Regarding the issue of "Dominion", **RABBI AVRAHAM YITZCHAK
KOOK** writes:

❙❙There is no doubt to any intelligent and insightful
person that the 'dominion' mentioned in THE TORAH

is not referring to the rulership of a despot who is cruel to his nation and workers with the sole intent of deriving his own personal gains and desires. Heaven forbid that such a revolting rule of slavery should be eternally imprinted in **God**'s world - who is good to all and merciful towards all His creations and who said, '**Let a world of kindness be built! -** עוֹלָם חֶסֶד יִבָּנֶה' (Psalms 89:3)"

(The vision of vegetarianism and peace)

Rabbi Yitzchak Hebenstreit:

❝If one is meritorious, they are granted dominion over animals. If they are not meritorious, animals have dominion over them; and this is stated in Bereshit (9:2): '**And your fear and terror will be upon every wild beast of the earth -** וּמוֹרַאֲכֶם וְחִתְּכֶם יִהְיֶה עַל כָּל־חַיַּת הָאָרֶץ'.

And in tractate Shabbat 151 it says: 'An animal does not rule over a human until the human appears to the animal as one of its own', as the verse in Psalms (49:13) states: '**Man does not abide in honor; he is like the beasts that perish -** וְאָדָם בִּיקָר בַּל־יָלִין נִמְשַׁל כַּבְּהֵמוֹת נִדְמוּ'.

This implies that as long as one follows the will of God, animals do not rule over them.

Isaiah prophesizes about the future (11:8-9):

'**And an infant shall play over the hole of a snake and over the hole of an adder a weaned child shall stretch forth his hand. They shall neither harm nor destroy on all My holy mount, for the land shall be full of knowledge of the Lord as water covers the sea -** וְשִׁעֲשַׁע

יוֹנֵק עַל־חֻר פָּתֶן וְעַל מְאוּרַת צִפְעוֹנִי גָּמוּל יָדוֹ הָדָה: לֹא־יָרֵעוּ וְלֹא־יַשְׁחִיתוּ בְּכָל־הַר קָדְשִׁי כִּי־מָלְאָה הָאָרֶץ דֵּעָה אֶת־יְ-הוָה כַּמַּיִם לַיָּם מְכַסִּים׳.

This goodness will come in a generation that is filled with knowledge and does not consume meat, because in this future time even carnivorous animals will no longer tear into their prey, as the lion and cattle will eat straw, as written (Isaiah 11:6-7): 'And a wolf shall live with a lamb, and a leopard shall lie with a kid; and a calf and a lion cub and a fatling [shall lie] together, and a small child shall lead them. And a cow and a bear shall graze and together their children shall lie; and a lion, like cattle, shall eat straw - וְגָר זְאֵב עִם־כֶּבֶשׂ וְנָמֵר עִם־גְּדִי יִרְבָּץ וְעֵגֶל וּכְפִיר וּמְרִיא יַחְדָּו וְנַעַר קָטֹן נֹהֵג בָּם: וּפָרָה וָדֹב תִּרְעֶינָה יַחְדָּו יִרְבְּצוּ יַלְדֵיהֶן וְאַרְיֵה כַּבָּקָר יֹאכַל־תֶּבֶן׳.

If there is no full proof of this, there is at least a hint to it in the book of **DANIEL**, when **DANIEL** was in the lion's den and **GOD** closed the mouths of the lions and they did not harm him. It was because **DANIEL** did not eat the flesh of animals, thus the animal did not eat his flesh. As specifically stated in **DANIEL**, he tells the chief officer not to give him any of the 'King's food' which included meat. Rather, he requested seeds, which are vegetation and do not involve spillage of blood. It is for a good reason that he is called (Daniel 10:11) 'Daniel, the man of charms - דָּנִיֵּאל אִישׁ חֲמוּדוֹת׳.

Let us return to the previous topic. **RABBI CHANINA BEN DOSA** was a vegetarian and did not eat meat. He ate only grains, vegetation and fruit from trees. This is stated in THE TALMUD (TAANIT 24):

'The entire world is sustained by the merit of My son CHANINA BEN DOSA, and yet for CHANINA, my son, a kav (small portion) of carobs, is sufficient to sustain him for an entire week, from one SHABBAT to the next SHABBAT'.

From here we see that RABBI CHANINA BEN DOSA did not spill innocent blood and did not satisfy himself by destroying others. He was satisfied with carob, which is but 'Dew from heaven and fat of the land - מִטַּל הַשָּׁמַיִם וּמִשְׁמַנֵּי הָאָרֶץ' (Bereshit 27:28). This is consistent with his philosophy (PIRKEI AVOT 3:10) that 'One who is pleasing to GOD's creations is pleasing to GOD'. The inference from the term 'creations' instead of 'people', is all living beings.

Now, the words of THE TALMUD are not difficult to understand, if we come to wonder: how did RABBI CHANINA BEN DOSA endanger himself by relying upon a miracle when in great and impending danger? RABBI CHANINA BEN DOSA never killed or hurt any living creature. He was certain that the ARVAD (snake) would not harm him since he knew that it is not the ARVAD (snake) that can kill but rather the sin, and even though it was possible that he was guilty of some sin; 'For there is no righteous person upon earth who has done good but not sinned - כִּי אָדָם אֵין צַדִּיק בָּאָרֶץ אֲשֶׁר יַעֲשֶׂה־טּוֹב וְלֹא יֶחֱטָא' (ECCLESIASTES [KOHELET] 7:20).

Moreover, the Satan accuses at a time of danger and specifically against righteous people whom GOD judges strictly. But regarding cruelty and the spillage of blood he was certain he was free of iniquity, and he knew that punishment is meted out measure for measure; and since he reflected upon his actions with regard to Tza'ar Ba'alei Chayim and spilling their blood and found no iniquity, he did not fear the Arvad (snake), because it is not the Arvad (snake) that kills, rather it is sin".

(Rabbi Yitzchak Hebenstreit: book Kivroth hatta'avah)

Rabbi Moshe ben Gershom Chefetz:

❙❙It makes good sense to accept the idea that He who with kindness supervises all humans, would also supervise all of His creations; and if not, why did He create the numerous and varied animals, birds and insects? Were they all created for man's benefit? This would be a foolish idea! Many creatures have an abhorrence for humans and are a bother and some are of no consequence to man. A wholesome individual is satisfied with a little bread and water and has no need to hunt animals for his enjoyment, which is the opposite of what was intended for our souls". (Melechet Machashevet, Parashat Noach)

In Jewish law not only do humans stand trial and bear punishment; animals do as well. We see in our sages' words a philosophy claiming that animals bear responsibility for their actions. The Talmud in tractate Sanhedrin requires having 23 judges for a court (a small Sanhedrin) to execute capital punishment upon a guilty animal.

MAIMONIDES:

> ❚❚A capital court is constituted with no less than 23 people and is termed 'THE SMALL SANHEDRIN', whether judging a human or an animal; therefore, we do not judge an ox to be stoned or an animal that has been party to bestiality with less than 23. Even a lion, bear, leopard or cheetah that are domesticated and have owners and have killed, they are judged with 23. But a snake that has killed, one can kill it".
>
> (MAIMONIDES, HILCHOT SANHEDRIN 5:3)

Explicit and practical reference to the goal and purpose of animals in our world is found in **RAMBAM**'s words, and I will bring them in their entirety:

> ❚❚I consider therefore the following opinion as the most correct opinion according to the teaching of THE TORAH, and best in accordance with the results of philosophy; namely, that one **should not believe** that the Universe exists for man's sake, but that each being exists for its own sake and not for anything else [...] every being lives for the sake of its own existence.
>
> [...] As you study the book which leads all who want to be instructed of the truth, and is therefore called TORAH (which literally means 'Instruction'), you will comprehend from the beginning of the account of the Creation to its end the opinion which we attempt to expound, that no part of the creation is described as being in existence for the sake of another part [...]

You must not be misled by what is stated of the stars [that **God** put them in the firmament of the heavens] 'To give light upon the earth. And to rule by day and by night - לְהָאִיר עַל־הָאָרֶץ: וְלִמְשֹׁל בַּיּוֹם וּבַלַּיְלָה' (Bereshit 1:17-18). You might perhaps think that this is a statement of their purpose. This is not the case; we are only informed of the nature of the stars, which **God** desired to create with such properties that they should be able to give light and to rule. In a similar manner we must understand the passage referring to man, 'and dominate the fish of the sea, the birds of the heaven, and every living thing that moves upon the earth - וּרְדוּ בִּדְגַת הַיָּם וּבְעוֹף הַשָּׁמַיִם וּבְכָל־חַיָּה הָרֹמֶשֶׂת עַל־הָאָרֶץ' (Bereshit, 1:28). Here too it is not meant to say that man was created for this purpose, but only that this was the nature which **God** gave man.

[…] Similarly, a certain citizen may imagine that it is the purpose of the king to protect his house by night from thieves. To some extent this is correct: for when his house is protected, and he has derived this benefit through the king who rules the country, it appears as if it were the purpose of the king to protect the house of that man.

In this manner we must explain every verse of which the literal meaning would imply that something superior was created for the sake of something inferior, which is to say that it is part of the nature of the superior thing [to influence the inferior in a certain manner]. We remain firm in our belief that the whole universe was created in accordance with the will of **God**, and we do not inquire for any other cause or object.

Just as we do not ask what is the purpose of **GOD**'s existence, so we do not ask what was the object of His will, which is the cause of the existence of all things with their present properties, both those that have been created and those that will be created.

[…] This must be our belief when we have a correct knowledge of our own self, and comprehend the true nature of everything; we must be content, and not trouble our mind with seeking a certain final cause for things that have none, or have no other final cause but their own existence, which stems from the Will of **GOD**, or, if you prefer, on the Divine Wisdom".

(MOREH NEVUCHIM - GUIDE FOR THE PERPLEXED, 3:13)

In a different chapter **RAMBAM** writes,

❚❚ Know that the difficulties which lead to confusion in the question what is the purpose of the Universe or of any of its parts, originate from man having an erroneous idea of himself, and believes that the whole world exists only for his sake.   (MOREH NEVUCHIM - GUIDE FOR THE PERPLEXED, 3:25)

"SINCE HE WAS COMPASSIONATE, WE SHALL BE COMPASSIONATE ON HIM"

"R EBBI's[12] suffering was the result of an incident which he brought upon himself, and through a subsequent event his suffering went away.

What was the first incident that brought on his suffering?

12   When ever it says "REBBI", it refers to RABBI YEHUDAH HANASI.

A calf was being led to slaughter. It hung its head on the corner of **Rabbi Yehuda HaNasi**'s garment and cried. **Rebbi** said to the calf, "Go, for you were created for this purpose".

Then it was said in Heaven: "Since he was not compassionate towards the calf, let afflictions come upon him".

The incident that removed the suffering is that one day, the maidservant of **Rabbi Yehuda HaNasi** was sweeping his house. There were young weasels lying about, and she was in the process of sweeping them out.

Rabbi Yehuda HaNasi said to her: "Let them be, as it is written (Psalms 145:9): 'And His mercies are over all His creations - וְרַחֲמָיו עַל־כָּל־מַעֲשָׂיו'".

It was then said in heaven: "Since he was compassionate, we shall be compassionate on him, and he was relieved of his suffering". (Bavli, Bava Metzia 85a)

Regarding **Rebbi**'s suffering, the head of the Lublin Court, **Rabbi Eliyahu Kletzkin** states:

> ❚❚ Our holy Rabbi was punished because he said '**Go, as you were created for this purpose**', as if the calf was only created for man's consumption and desire and not for its own sake". (Responsa Imrei Shefer, siman 34)

The Geonim were the heads of **Yeshivot** in **Sura** and **Pumpadita** in **Babylonia** and in **the kand of Israel**. They were the highest ranking lawmakers after the completion of **the Talmud**.

RAV SHRIRA GAON, RAV HAI GAON and one of the students of THE GEONIM, RAV YITZCHAK ALFASI wrote on this incident concerning REBBI YEHUDA HANASI and the suffering he endured after saying those words to the calf:

"Clearly, the calf was **not** created for slaughter".

(TESHUVOT HAGEONIM [EDITOR: AVRAHAM ELIYAHU HARKAVI], SIMAN 375)

RABBI YITZCHAK HEBENSTREIT:

❝Let us look deeply and understand the individual who suffers, difficult suffering such as sickness and afflictions causing one to shout in pain. Sometimes, those who visit the sick person ask: how can it be that the Master of the Universe who is merciful and kind does not have mercy on this poor person when he hears his cries? How can The Healer of the sick listen to the supplications of this poor person and not act mercifully to heal him? The voice of his suffering is heard in heaven! But where is the compassion and a measure of mercy?

If we look at the deeds of humans with an open eye and understand the characteristics of **GOD**, it will not be difficult to see that a general rule is that good and bad do not come from **GOD**, rather man causes it all himself. All is placed in man's hands, be it bad or good. As a result of his misdeeds he brings unto himself evil. Conversely, by doing good he brings good unto himself, as is written in the verse (BOOK OF LAMENTATIONS [EICHA] 3:38-39): **'By the command of the Lord neither good nor evil come. Why should a living man complain?** - מִפִּי עֶלְיוֹן לֹא תֵצֵא הָרָעוֹת

'וְהַטּוֹב: מַה־יִּתְאוֹנֵן אָדָם חָי גֶּבֶר עַל־חֲטָאָיו'. The meaning of this is that bad and good do not come from **God** but emanate from man's deeds. If one would reflect on their misdeeds, they'd realize that they bring suffering upon themselves and it is incumbent upon them to consider the sin and the reason that bad has befallen them. They must focus their heart on understanding what brought about the difficulties, as the verse states (Berachot 5):

'If a person sees that suffering has befallen him, he should examine his actions'.

Let one investigate and analyze to determine which sin has brought upon him this suffering. When one realizes which sin they committed they can then return to **God** in wholesome repentance. Only then can the sick heal from their illness and return to their original state, as it says (Nedarim 41):

'The sick does not recover from their illness until all their sins are atoned'.

But how can a person know which sin caused bad to befall upon them? One should therefore note this general rule stated by our sages (Sanhedrin 90) 'According to how you judge others, heaven judges you'. Thus, if we see great difficulties coming to a person without mercy or kindness, this is measure for measure; since they act with cruelty towards others who are weaker than them and have no mercy towards them nor heed their shouts and cries. One must therefore examine their misdeeds to see if there is an analogue to their misfortune.

This concept will assist us in understanding the incident with **RABBI YEHUDA HANASI** (BAVA METZIA 85). This event brought upon him suffering and as the result of another event his suffering went away. One time a calf was being led to slaughter and tucked its head under **REBBI**'s coat and cried to him as if saying, 'REBBI! Save me from them!' But **REBBI** pushed the calf and said to it, 'For this you have been created'. Heaven said, 'Since he was not merciful to the calf, let suffering befall him'. and **REBBI** suffered for thirteen years. And because of the second incident the suffering ceased. One day his maid was cleaning the house and when sweeping she came upon weasels and wanted to throw them outside. **REBBI** said, 'Let them be', quoting the verse (Psalms 145:9), '**God is merciful upon all of His creations - וְרַחֲמָיו עַל־כָּל־ מַעֲשָׂיו**'. They said above in heaven, 'Since he was merciful to **GOD**'s creations, let us also be merciful to him'. Only then did **REBBI**'s thirteen yearlong pain heal. Let this incident be the strong basis upon which this topic rests and open your eyes to see! Who is greater than our holy **REBBI**? From the days of **MOSHE** until **REBBI** we do not find anyone who merited sitting at two tables. And if this befell a great man like our holy **REBBI**, what can we expect for ourselves? During those thirteen years **REBBI** prayed to **GOD** and poured forth requests before Him. Still, they did not help at all until he addressed that specific sin for which he was smitten. It was only when he repented and repaired the sin and that specific trait by reversing his actions of pushing the calf towards slaughter and not having mercy upon it and not hearing its cry and not saving it from those coming after it. Therefore, by necessity the repentance must be in accordance with the sin, acting mercifully. Therefore, he was not healed until he had mercy upon **God**'s creations and saved the weasels from the one chasing them and recited the verse '**He is merciful towards all His creations** - 'וְרַחֲמָיו עַל־כָּל־מַעֲשָׂיו' (Psalms 145:9). Thus we see, 'One who is merciful towards **God**'s creations, heaven is merciful towards him'.

I have found a story from a wise person who personally witnessed it. When they took a young calf from its mother, the mother cried with a bitter voice as if she was asking them to bring her precious baby back and nothing calmed her. The cruel butcher, 'the partner of Amalek', murdered the calf, skinned it and hung its hide on the wall of the dairy barn so it would dry quickly. When the mother cow saw the skin, she recognized it as the fruit of her womb and gave out a shout that was truly long and bitter. The unfortunate mother whose hope was lost forever and had no comfort approached the wall and licked the hide of her child, put her lips to it and groaned, licked it and cried as long as the hide was hanging there.

One should no longer wonder, then, why at times very bad and unmerciful things befall a person. Isn't it easy to understand that because of cruel deeds like this, a person causes measure for measure to befall upon himselves? The way one acts towards others is the way Heaven acts towards him. This means that a person determines whether they receive bad or good, because the general rule is: all who show mercy to His creations, Heaven is merciful towards them. And the reverse is also true: those who don't have mercy on GOD's creations, Heaven is not merciful towards them. This is written clearly in an explicit verse (PSALMS 18:26-27): 'With a kind one be kind, with a sincere one be sincere. With a pure one be pure, but with a crooked one you deal crookedly - עִם־חָסִיד תִּתְחַסָּד עִם־גְּבַר תָּמִים תִּתַּמָּם: עִם־נָבָר תִּתְבָּרָר וְעִם־עִקֵּשׁ תִּתְפַּתָּל'. So, if one wants to prevent bad things from happening to himself, he should not do to others what he does not want done to him. As the sage Hillel taught: what is distasteful to you, do not do to others! One should not only distance oneself totally from cruelty, but even prefer to suffer rather than bring suffering upon others. And all who resist their inappropriate urges, Heaven forgives them for their iniquities.

(RABBI YITZCHAK HEBENSTREIT: BOOK KIVROTH HATTA'AVAH)

RABBI YITZCHAK KARO (the uncle of RABBI YOSEF KARO):

❝ The verse (PSALMS 145:16), 'You open up Your hand and satisfy the desire of every living thing - פּוֹתֵחַ אֶת־יָדֶךָ וּמַשְׂבִּיעַ לְכָל־חַי רָצוֹן', refers to animals who have no ability to speak yet have desires. Furthermore, creatures have likeness to GOD who knows every small detail and looks after them. **This is the secret of TZA'AR BA'ALEI CHAYIM from THE TORAH [...] it is written (PSALMS 36:7):**

> 'A man and animal you save, God - אָדָם־וּבְהֵמָה תּוֹשִׁיעַ
> יְ־הֹוָה'. A man, by the merit of animals, will be saved
> by **God**; as **God**, The master of nature, gives rain
> for the benefit of animals". (Toldot Yitzchak, Vayikra 25)

In biblical times when the divine presence was apparent in Israel, humans and animals lived together and participated in each other's anguish. For instance, in the Book of Jonah we find that at a time of difficulty animals and humans gather together and call to **God** to be saved: "They covered themselves with sackcloth, man and beast, and called loudly to God - וַיִּתְכַּסּוּ שַׂקִּים הָאָדָם וְהַבְּהֵמָה וַיִּקְרְאוּ אֶל־אֱ־לֹהִים בְּחָזְקָה". (Jonah 3:8) And the verse says, "Now should I not take pity on Nineveh, the great city, in which there are many more than one hundred twenty thousand people who do not know their right hand from their left, and many beasts as well? - וַאֲנִי לֹא אָחוּס עַל־ נִינְוֵה הָעִיר הַגְּדוֹלָה אֲשֶׁר יֶשׁ־בָּהּ הַרְבֵּה מִשְׁתֵּים־עֶשְׂרֵה רִבּוֹ אָדָם אֲשֶׁר לֹא־יָדַע בֵּין־יְמִינוֹ לִשְׂמֹאלוֹ וּבְהֵמָה רַבָּה" (Jonah 4:11). **God**'s concern for animals was known to them and they honored it, as it says "The beasts of the field shall honor Me, the jackals and the ostriches - תְּכַבְּדֵנִי חַיַּת הַשָּׂדֶה תַּנִּים וּבְנוֹת יַעֲנָה". (Isaiah 43, 20)

PEREK SHIRA
(CHAPTER OF SONG)

"הַחַיָּה וְכָל בְּהֵמָה רֶמֶשׂ וְצִפּוֹר כָּנָף׃" (תְּהִלִּים קמ״ח, י׳)

"All wild and tamed beasts, creeping things and winged birds". (PSALMS 148:10)

PEREK SHIRA is attributed to KING DAVID and it depicts the song of the animals to their Creator, as we recite in on the SHABBAT PRAYER (NISHMAT KOL CHAI): "The soul of every living being shall bless Your name, Lord our God; and the spirit of all flesh shall always glorify and exalt Your remembrance, our King – נִשְׁמַת כָּל חַי תְּבָרֵךְ אֶת שִׁמְךָ ה' אֱ-לֹהֵינוּ, וְרוּחַ כָּל בָּשָׂר תְּפָאֵר וּתְרוֹמֵם אֶת שִׁמְךָ מַלְכֵּנוּ תָּמִיד."

Many books were written with wonderful commentary on PEREK SHIRA such as 'ZIMRAT HA'ARETZ', 'BIRKAT AVRAHAM' and others. Since our topic is the purpose of animals, I have copied their songs out of PEREK SHIRA:

It is taught that **RABBI ELIEZER** said: Anyone who occupies himself with PEREK SHIRA in this world merits to recite it in the World to Come and is delivered from calamity, and from the Evil Inclination, and from severe judgment, and from the SATAN, and from all types of evil and destruction.

"Study with all your heart and with all your soul to know My ways and to be diligent at the doors of My Torah. Keep My Torah in your heart, and reverence of Me should be before your eyes. Guard your mouth from all transgression and purify and sanctify yourself from all fault and iniquity, and I will be with you everywhere" (BERACHOT 17a).

"Everything that the Holy One, Blessed be He, created in this world, He created only for His honor, as it says (ISAIAH 43:7): **'Every one that is called by My name, and whom I have created for My honor, I have formed him, yes, I have made him** - כֹּל הַנִּקְרָא בִשְׁמִי וְלִכְבוֹדִי בְּרָאתִיו יְצַרְתִּיו אַף־עֲשִׂיתִיו**"** (AVOT 6:11).

REBBI YEHUDA HANASI said, "Anyone who engrosses

himself in PEREK SHIRA in this world merits to learn and to teach, to observe and to fulfill and to perform (TORAH and MITZVOT), and his learning succeeds, and he is delivered from the Evil Inclination and from all harm, and from castigation of the grave and from the verdict of GEHENNOM, and from the birth pangs of MESSIAH, and enjoys longevity of days, and merits life in the World-to-Come".

It is taught that **RABBI ELIEZER** said: "Anyone who recites PEREK SHIRA in this world merits to recite it in the World to Come, for it is written, '**Then Moshe shall sing -** אָז יָשִׁיר־מֹשֶׁה' (SHEMOT 9:1) — it does not say 'sang' (past tense), but '**shall sing**' (future tense), meaning in the World to Come. (see SANHEDRIN 41b)

תַּרְנְגוֹל אוֹמֵר: בְּשָׁעָה שֶׁבָּא הַקָּדוֹשׁ בָּרוּךְ הוּא אֵצֶל הַצַּדִּיקִים בְּגַן עֵדֶן, זוֹלְפִים כָּל אִילָנֵי גַּן עֵדֶן בְּשָׂמִים וּמְרַנְּנִים וּמְשַׁבְּחִים, וְאָז גַּם הוּא מִתְעוֹרֵר וּמְשַׁבֵּחַ:

THE ROOSTER is saying: "When the blessed Holy One comes to the righteous in the Garden of Eden, all the trees in the Garden of Eden scatter their spices, and they rejoice and praise, and then It (the rooster) too is aroused and praises".

בְּקוֹל רִאשׁוֹן אוֹמֵר: שְׂאוּ שְׁעָרִים | רָאשֵׁיכֶם וְהִנָּשְׂאוּ פִּתְחֵי עוֹלָם וְיָבוֹא מֶלֶךְ הַכָּבוֹד: מִי זֶה מֶלֶךְ הַכָּבוֹד יְ־הֹוָה עִזּוּז וְגִבּוֹר יְ־הֹוָה גִּבּוֹר מִלְחָמָה: (תהלים כ״ד, ז׳-ח׳)

IN FIRST CALL IT SAYS: "O gates, lift up your heads! Up high, you everlasting doors, so the King of glory may come in! Who is the King of glory? the LORD, mighty and valiant, the LORD, valiant in battle".   (Psalms 24:7-8)

בְּקוֹל שֵׁנִי אוֹמֵר: שְׂאוּ שְׁעָרִים | רָאשֵׁיכֶם וּשְׂאוּ פִּתְחֵי עוֹלָם וְיָבֹא מֶלֶךְ הַכָּבוֹד: מִי הוּא זֶה מֶלֶךְ הַכָּבוֹד יְ־הֹוָה צְבָאוֹת הוּא מֶלֶךְ הַכָּבוֹד סֶלָה: (תהלים כ״ד, ט׳-י׳)

IN SECOND CALL IT SAYS: "O gates, lift up your heads! Lift them up, you everlasting doors, so the King of glory may come in! Who is the King of glory? the LORD of hosts, He is the King of glory! Selah".   (Psalms 24:9-10)

בְּקוֹל שְׁלִישִׁי אוֹמֵר: עִמְדוּ צַדִּיקִים וְעִסְקוּ בַּתּוֹרָה כְּדֵי שֶׁיִּהְיֶה שְׂכַרְכֶם כָּפוּל לָעוֹלָם הַבָּא:

IN ITS THIRD CALL IT SAYS: "Stand, O righteous ones, and engross yourselves in Torah so that your reward will be double in the World-to-Come".

בְּקוֹל רְבִיעִי אוֹמֵר: לִישׁוּעָתְךָ קִוִּיתִי יְ־הֹוָה: (בראשית מ״ט, י״ח)

IN ITS FOURTH CALL IT SAYS: "For your deliverance, I wait, Adonay".   (BERESHIT 49:18)

בְּקוֹל חֲמִישִׁי אוֹמֵר: עַד־מָתַי עָצֵל | תִּשְׁכָּב מָתַי תָּקוּם מִשְּׁנָתֶךָ: (משלי ו׳, ט׳)

IN ITS FIFTH CALL IT SAYS: "How long will you lie there, lazybones; When will you wake from your sleep?"

(Proverbs 6:9)

בְּקוֹל שִׁשִּׁי אוֹמֵר: אַל־תֶּאֱהַב שֵׁנָה פֶּן־תִּוָּרֵשׁ פְּקַח עֵינֶיךָ שְׂבַע־לָחֶם:

(מִשְׁלֵי כ', י"ג)

IN ITS SIXTH CALL IT SAYS: "Do not love sleep lest you be impoverished; Keep your eyes open and you will have plenty of food".

(Proverbs 20:13)

בְּקוֹל שְׁבִיעִי אוֹמֵר: עֵת לַעֲשׂוֹת לַי־הֹוָה הֵפֵרוּ תּוֹרָתֶךָ:

(תְּהִלִּים קי"ט, קכ"ו)

IN ITS SEVENTH CALL IT SAYS: "It is a time to act for the LORD, for they have violated Your teaching".

(Psalms 119:126)

תַּרְנְגֹלֶת אוֹמֶרֶת: נֹתֵן לֶחֶם לְכָל־בָּשָׂר כִּי לְעוֹלָם חַסְדּוֹ:

(תְּהִלִּים קל"ו, כ"ה)

THE HEN SAYS: "Who gives food to all flesh, His steadfast love is eternal".

(Psalms 136:25)

יוֹנָה אוֹמֶרֶת: כְּסוּס עָגוּר כֵּן אֲצַפְצֵף אֶהְגֶּה כַּיּוֹנָה דַּלּוּ עֵינַי לַמָּרוֹם אֲדֹנָי עָשְׁקָה־לִּי עָרְבֵנִי:

(יְשַׁעְיָה ל"ח, י"ד)

THE PIGEON SAYS: "I piped like a swift or a swallow, I moaned like a dove, As my eyes, all worn, looked to heaven: "My Lord, I am in straits; Be my surety!".

(Isaiah 38:14)

אוֹמֶרֶת **יוֹנָה** לִפְנֵי הַקָּדוֹשׁ בָּרוּךְ הוּא: רִבּוֹנוֹ שֶׁל עוֹלָם, יִהְיוּ מְזוֹנוֹתַי
מְרוֹרִים כַּזַּיִת בְּיָדֶךָ, וְאַל יִהְיוּ מְתוּקִים כִּדְבַשׁ עַל יְדֵי בָּשָׂר וָדָם:

THE **PIGEON** SAYS in front of The Holy One, Blessed
be He: "Master of the World, may my sustenance be
as bitter as an olive in Your hands, rather than bring
sweet as honey in the hands of flesh and blood".

נֶשֶׁר אוֹמֵר: וְאַתָּה יְ־הֹוָה־אֱ־לֹהִים ׀ צְבָאוֹת אֱ־לֹהֵי יִשְׂרָאֵל
הָקִיצָה לִפְקֹד כָּל־הַגּוֹיִם אַל־תָּחֹן כָּל־בֹּגְדֵי אָוֶן סֶלָה: (תהלים נ"ט, ו')

THE **EAGLE** SAYS: "You, O LORD God of hosts, God of
Israel, bestir Yourself to bring all nations to account;
have no mercy on any treacherous villain. Selah".

(Psalms 59:6)

עָגוּר אוֹמֵר: הוֹדוּ לַי־הֹוָה בְּכִנּוֹר בְּנֵבֶל עָשׂוֹר זַמְּרוּ־לוֹ: תהלים ל"ג, ב')

THE **CRANE** SAYS: "Praise the LORD with the lyre; with
the ten-stringed harp sing to Him".   (Psalms 33:2)

צִפּוֹר אוֹמֵר: גַּם־צִפּוֹר ׀ מָצְאָה בַיִת וּדְרוֹר ׀ קֵן לָהּ אֲשֶׁר־שָׁתָה
אֶפְרֹחֶיהָ אֶת־מִזְבְּחוֹתֶיךָ יְ־הֹוָה צְבָאוֹת מַלְכִּי וֵא־לֹהָי: (תהלים פ"ד, ד')

THE **BIRD** SAYS: "Even the sparrow has found a home,
and the swallow a nest for herself in which to set her
young, near Your altar, O LORD of hosts, my king and
my God".   (Psalms 84:4)

סְנוּנִית אוֹמֶרֶת: לְמַעַן ׀ יְזַמֶּרְךָ כָבוֹד וְלֹא יִדֹּם יְ־הֹוָה אֱ־לֹהַי
לְעוֹלָם אוֹדֶךָ:   (תהלים ל', י"ג)

THE **SWALLOW** SAYS: "That [my] whole being might sing hymns to You endlessly; O LORD my God, I will praise You forever". (Psalms 30:13)

טָסִית אוֹמֶרֶת: עֶזְרִי מֵעִם יְ־הֹוָה עֹשֵׂה שָׁמַיִם וָאָרֶץ: (תְּהִלִּים קכ״א, ב׳)

THE **SWIFT** SAYS: "My help comes from the LORD, maker of heaven and earth". (Psalms 121:2)

צִיָּה אוֹמֶרֶת: אוֹר זָרֻעַ לַצַּדִּיק וּלְיִשְׁרֵי־לֵב שִׂמְחָה: (תְּהִלִּים צ״ז, י״א)

THE **PETREL** SAYS: "Light is sown for the righteous, radianceb for the upright". (Psalms 97:11)

רְצְפִי אוֹמֵר: נַחֲמוּ נַחֲמוּ עַמִּי יֹאמַר אֱ־לֹהֵיכֶם: (יְשַׁעְיָה מ׳, א׳)

THE **BAT** SAYS: "Comfort, oh comfort My people, Says your God". (Isaiah 1:40)

חֲסִידָה אוֹמֶרֶת: דַּבְּרוּ עַל־לֵב יְרוּשָׁלַ͏ִם וְקִרְאוּ אֵלֶיהָ כִּי מָלְאָה צְבָאָהּ כִּי נִרְצָה עֲוֹנָהּ כִּי לָקְחָה מִיַּד יְ־הֹוָה כִּפְלַיִם בְּכָל־חַטֹּאתֶיהָ: (יְשַׁעְיָהמ׳, ב׳)

THE **STORK** SAYS: "Speak tenderly to Jerusalem, And declare to her That her term of service is over, That her iniquity is expiated; For she has received at the hand of the LORD Double for all her sins". (Isaiah 40:2)

עוֹרֵב אוֹמֵר: מִי יָכִין לָעֹרֵב צֵידוֹ כִּי־יְלָדָיו אֶל־אֵ־ל יְשַׁוֵּעוּ יִתְעוּ לִבְלִי־אֹכֶל: (אִיּוֹב ל״ח, מ״א)

THE **CROW** SAYS: "Who provides food for the raven When his young cry out to God And wander about without food?" (Job 38:41)

זַרְזִיר אוֹמֵר: וְנוֹדַע בַּגּוֹיִם זַרְעָם וְצֶאֱצָאֵיהֶם בְּתוֹךְ הָעַמִּים

כָּל־רֹאֵיהֶם יַכִּירוּם כִּי הֵם זֶרַע בֵּרַךְ יְ־הֹוָה: (יְשַׁעְיָה ס״א, ט׳)

THE **STARLING** SAYS: "Their offspring shall be known among the nations, Their descendants in the midst of the peoples. All who see them shall recognize That they are a stock the LORD has blessed". (Isaiah 61:9)

אַוָּז שֶׁבַּבַּיִת אוֹמֶרֶת: הוֹדוּ לַי־הֹוָה קִרְאוּ בִשְׁמוֹ הוֹדִיעוּ בָעַמִּים

עֲלִילוֹתָיו: שִׁירוּ־לוֹ זַמְּרוּ־לוֹ שִׂיחוּ בְּכָל־נִפְלְאוֹתָיו: (תְּהִלִּים ק״ה, א׳)

THE **DOMESTIC GOOSE** SAYS: "Praise the LORD; call on His name; proclaim His deeds among the peoples".

(Psalms 105:1-2)

אַוָּז הַבָּר הַמְשׁוֹטֶטֶת בַּמִּדְבָּר, כְּשֶׁרוֹאָה אֶת יִשְׂרָאֵל עוֹסְקִים בַּתּוֹרָה

אוֹמֶרֶת: קוֹל קוֹרֵא בַּמִּדְבָּר פַּנּוּ דֶּרֶךְ יְ־הֹוָה יַשְּׁרוּ בָּעֲרָבָה מְסִלָּה

לֵא־לֹהֵינוּ: (יְשַׁעְיָה מ׳, ג׳)

THE **WILD GOOSE** that flies in the wilderness, when it sees Israel engrossed in **TORAH** says: "A voice rings out: 'Clear in the desert A road for the LORD! Level in the wilderness A highway for our God!'" (Isaiah 40:3)

וְעַל מְצִיאוּת מְזוֹנוֹתֶיהָ בַּמִּדְבָּר אוֹמֶרֶת: ...אָרוּר הַגֶּבֶר אֲשֶׁר יִבְטַח

בָּאָדָם...: בָּרוּךְ הַגֶּבֶר אֲשֶׁר יִבְטַח בַּי־הֹוָה וְהָיָה יְ־הֹוָה מִבְטַחוֹ:

(יִרְמְיָה י״ז, ה׳, ז׳)

AND UPON FINDING ITS FOOD IN THE DESERT IT SAYS: "Cursed is he who trusts in man ... Blessed is he who trusts in the LORD, Whose trust is the LORD alone".

(JEREMIAH 17: 5, 7)

פְּרוֹגִיוֹת אוֹמְרִים: בִּטְחוּ בַי־הֹוָה עֲדֵי־עַד כִּי בְּיָהּ יְ־הֹוָה צוּר עוֹלָמִים: (יְשַׁעְיָה כ״ו, ד׳)

THE **D**UCKS SAY: "Trust in the LORD for ever and ever, For in YAH the LORD you have an everlasting Rock".

(Isaiah 26:4)

רָחֲמָה אוֹמֶרֶת: אֶשְׁרְקָה לָהֶם וַאֲקַבְּצֵם כִּי פְדִיתִים וְרָבוּ כְּמוֹ רָבוּ: (זְכַרְיָה י׳, ח׳)

THE **B**EE-**E**ATER SAYS: "I will whistle to them and gather them, For I will redeem them; They shall increase band continue increasing". (Zechariah 10:8)

צִפֹּרַת כְּרָמִים אוֹמֶרֶת: אֶשָּׂא עֵינַי אֶל־הֶהָרִים מֵאַיִן יָבֹא עֶזְרִי: (תְּהִלִּים קכ״א, א׳)

THE **G**RASSHOPPER SAYS: "I turn my eyes to the mountains; from where will my help come?"

(Psalms 121:1)

חָסִיל אוֹמֵר: יְ־הֹוָה אֱ־לֹהַי אַתָּה אֲרוֹמִמְךָ אוֹדֶה שִׁמְךָ כִּי עָשִׂיתָ פֶּלֶא עֵצוֹת מֵרָחוֹק אֱמוּנָה אֹמֶן: (יְשַׁעְיָה כ״ה, א׳)

THE **L**OCUST SAYS: "O LORD, You are my God; I will extol You, I will praise Your name. For You planned graciousnessa of old, Counsels of steadfast faithfulness".

(Isaiah 25:1)

שְׁמָמִית אוֹמֶרֶת: הַלְלוּהוּ בְּצִלְצְלֵי־שָׁמַע הַלְלוּהוּ בְּצִלְצְלֵי תְרוּעָה: (תְּהִלִּים ק״נ, ה׳)

The Spider says: "Praise Him with resounding cymbals; praise Him with loud-clashing cymbals".

(Psalms 150:5)

זְבוּב אוֹמֵר: בְּשָׁעָה שֶׁאֵין יִשְׂרָאֵל עוֹסְקִים בַּתּוֹרָה, קוֹל אֹמֵר קְרָא וְאָמַר מָה אֶקְרָא כָּל־הַבָּשָׂר חָצִיר וְכָל־חַסְדּוֹ כְּצִיץ הַשָּׂדֶה: יָבֵשׁ חָצִיר נָבֵל צִיץ כִּי רוּחַ יְהוָה נָשְׁבָה בּוֹ אָכֵן חָצִיר הָעָם: יָבֵשׁ חָצִיר נָבֵל צִיץ וּדְבַר־אֱ־לֹהֵינוּ יָקוּם לְעוֹלָם: (יְשַׁעְיָה מ׳, ו׳-ח׳)
בּוֹרֵא נִיב שְׂפָתָיִם שָׁלוֹם | שָׁלוֹם לָרָחוֹק וְלַקָּרוֹב
אָמַר יְהוָה וּרְפָאתִיו: (יְשַׁעְיָה נ״ז, י״ט)

The Fly says: When Israel is not engrossed in Torah: "A voice rings out: 'Proclaim!' Another asks, 'What shall I proclaim?' 'All flesh is grass, All its goodness like flowers of the field: Grass withers, flowers fade When the breath of the LORD blows on them. Indeed, man is but grass: Grass withers, flowers fade - But the word of our God is always fulfilled!'"

(Isaiah 40:6,8)

"Heartening, comforting words: It shall be well, Well with the far and the near - said the LORD - And I will heal him".

(Isaiah 57:19)

תַּנִּינִים אוֹמְרִים: הַלְלוּ אֶת־יְיָ־הוָה מִן־הָאָרֶץ תַּנִּינִים וְכָל־תְּהֹמוֹת: (תְּהִלִּים קמ״ח, ז׳)

The Giant Sea Creatures say: "Praise the LORD, O you who are on earth, all sea monsters and ocean depths".

(Psalms 148:7)

לִוְיָתָן אוֹמֵר: הוֹדוּ לַי־הֹוָה כִּי־טוֹב כִּי לְעוֹלָם חַסְדּוֹ: (תְּהִלִּים קל״ו, א׳)

THE **WHALE** SAYS: "Praise the LORD; for He is good, His steadfast love is eternal". (Psalms 136:1)

דָּגִים אוֹמְרִים: קוֹל יְ־הֹוָה עַל־הַמָּיִם אֵ־ל־הַכָּבוֹד הִרְעִים יְ־הֹוָה עַל־מַיִם רַבִּים: (תְּהִלִּים כ״ט, ג׳)

THE **FISH** SAY: "The voice of the LORD is over the waters; the God of glory thunders, the LORD, over the mighty waters". (Psalms 29:3)

צְפַרְדֵּעַ אוֹמֶרֶת: בָּרוּךְ שֵׁם כְּבוֹד מַלְכוּתוֹ לְעוֹלָם וָעֶד:

THE **FROG** SAYS: "Blessed is the Name of His glorious Kingdom forever and ever!" (Talmud, tractate PESACHim 56a)

בְּהֵמָה דַקָּה טְהוֹרָה אוֹמֶרֶת: מִי־כָמֹכָה בָּאֵלִם יְ־הֹוָה מִי כָּמֹכָה נֶאְדָּר בַּקֹּדֶשׁ נוֹרָא תְהִלֹּת עֹשֵׂה פֶלֶא: (שְׁמוֹת ט״ו, י״א)

THE **SHEEP AND GOATS** SAYS: "Who is like You among the mighty, Adonay! Who is like You, adorned in holiness, Awesome in praise, doing wonders?" (SHEMOT 15:11)

בְּהֵמָה גַסָּה טְהוֹרָה אוֹמֶרֶת: הַרְנִינוּ לֵא־לֹהִים עוּזֵּנוּ הָרִיעוּ לֵא־לֹהֵי יַעֲקֹב: (תְּהִלִּים פ״א, ב׳)

THE **CATTLE** SAYS: "Sing joyously to God, our strength; raise a shout for the God of Jacob". (Psalms 81:2)

בְּהֵמָה דַקָּה טְמֵאָה אוֹמֶרֶת: הֵיטִיבָה יְ־הֹוָה לַטּוֹבִים וְלִישָׁרִים בְּלִבּוֹתָם: (תְּהִלִּים קכ״ה, ד׳)

THE **PIG** SAYS: "Do good, O LORD, to the good, to the upright in heart". (Psalms 128:2)

בְּהֵמָה גַסָּה טְמֵאָה אוֹמֶרֶת: יְגִיעַ כַּפֶּיךָ כִּי תֹאכֵל אַשְׁרֶיךָ וְטוֹב לָךְ:

(תְּהִלִּים קכ״ח, ב׳)

THE **BEAST OF BURDEN** SAYS: "You shall enjoy the fruit of your labors; you shall be happy and you shall prosper". (Psalms 128:2)

גָּמָל אוֹמֵר: יְ־הֹוָה מִמָּרוֹם יִשְׁאָג וּמִמְּעוֹן קָדְשׁוֹ יִתֵּן קוֹלוֹ שָׁאֹג יִשְׁאַג עַל־נָוֵהוּ: (יִרְמְיָה כ״ה, ל׳)

THE **CAMEL** SAYS: "The LORD roars from on high, He makes His voice heard from His holy dwelling; He roars aloud over His [earthly] abode". (JEREMIAH 25:30)

סוּס אוֹמֵר: הִנֵּה כְעֵינֵי עֲבָדִים אֶל־יַד אֲדוֹנֵיהֶם כְּעֵינֵי שִׁפְחָה אֶל־יַד גְּבִרְתָּהּ כֵּן עֵינֵינוּ אֶל־יְ־הֹוָה אֱ־לֹהֵינוּ עַד שֶׁיְּחָנֵּנוּ: (תְּהִלִּים קכ״ג, ב׳)

THE **HORSE** SAYS: "As the eyes of slaves follow their master's hand, as the eyes of a slave-girl follow the hand of her mistress, so our eyes are toward the LORD our God, awaiting His favor". (Psalms 123:2)

פֶּרֶד אוֹמֵר: יוֹדוּךָ יְ־הֹוָה כָּל־מַלְכֵי־אָרֶץ כִּי שָׁמְעוּ אִמְרֵי־פִיךָ: (תְּהִלִּים קל״ח, ד׳)

THE **MULE** SAYS: "All the kings of the earth shall praise You, O LORD, for they have heard the words You spoke". (Psalms 138:4)

חֲמוֹר אוֹמֵר: לְךָ יְ־הֹוָה הַגְּדֻלָּה וְהַגְּבוּרָה וְהַתִּפְאֶרֶת וְהַנֵּצַח וְהַהוֹד כִּי־כֹל בַּשָּׁמַיִם וּבָאָרֶץ לְךָ יְ־הֹוָה הַמַּמְלָכָה וְהַמִּתְנַשֵּׂא לְכֹל | לְרֹאשׁ:

(דִּבְרֵי הַיָּמִים א׳ כ״ט, י״א)

THE **DONKEY** SAYS: "Yours, LORD, are greatness, might, splendor, triumph, and majesty - yes, all that is in heaven and on earth; to You, LORD, belong kingship and preeminence above all". (Chronicles I, 29:11)

שׁוֹר אוֹמֵר: אָז יָשִׁיר־מֹשֶׁה וּבְנֵי יִשְׂרָאֵל אֶת־הַשִּׁירָה הַזֹּאת לַי־הֹוָה וַיֹּאמְרוּ לֵאמֹר אָשִׁירָה לַי־הֹוָה כִּי־גָאֹה גָּאָה סוּס וְרֹכְבוֹ רָמָה בַיָּם:

(שְׁמוֹת ט״ו, א׳)

THE **OX** SAYS: "Then Moshe and the **B'NEI YISRAEL** sang this song to Adonay and they said, I will sing to Adonay for He is most high, horse and its rider He threw into the sea". (SHEMOT 15:1)

בָּרוּךְ הַטּוֹב וְהַמֵּטִיב: **חַיּוֹת הַשָּׂדֶה** אוֹמְרִים:

THE **WILD ANIMALS** SAY: "Blessed is the Good One Who does good".

צְבִי אוֹמֵר: וַאֲנִי | אָשִׁיר עֻזֶּךָ וַאֲרַנֵּן לַבֹּקֶר חַסְדֶּךָ כִּי־הָיִיתָ מִשְׂגָּב לִי וּמָנוֹס בְּיוֹם צַר־לִי: (תְּהִלִּים נ״ט, י״ז)

THE **DEER** SAYS: "But I will sing of Your strength, extol each morning Your faithfulness; for You have been my haven, a refuge in time of trouble". (Psalms 59:17)

פִּיל אוֹמֵר: מַה־גָּדְלוּ מַעֲשֶׂיךָ יְ־הֹוָה מְאֹד עָמְקוּ מַחְשְׁבֹתֶיךָ:

(תְּהִלִּים צ״ב, ו׳)

THE ELEPHANT SAYS: "How great are Your works, O LORD, how very subtlea Your designs!"   (Psalms 92:6)

אַרְיֵה אוֹמֵר: יְ־הֹוָה כַּגִּבּוֹר יֵצֵא כְּאִישׁ מִלְחָמוֹת יָעִיר קִנְאָה יָרִיעַ אַף־יַצְרִיחַ עַל־אֹיְבָיו יִתְגַּבָּר: (יְשַׁעְיָה מ״ב, י״ג)

THE LION SAYS: "The LORD goes forth like a warrior, Like a fighter He whips up His rage. He yells, He roars aloud, He charges upon His enemies".   (Isaiah 42:13)

דֹב אוֹמֵר: יִשְׂאוּ מִדְבָּר וְעָרָיו חֲצֵרִים תֵּשֵׁב קֵדָר יָרֹנּוּ יֹשְׁבֵי סֶלַע מֵרֹאשׁ הָרִים יִצְוָחוּ: יָשִׂימוּ לַי־הֹוָה כָּבוֹד וּתְהִלָּתוֹ בָּאִיִּים יַגִּידוּ:   (יְשַׁעְיָה מ״ב, י״א־י״ב)

THE BEAR SAYS: "Let the desert and its towns cry aloud, The villages where Kedar dwells; Let Sela's inhabitants shout, Call out from the peaks of the mountains. Let them do honor to the LORD, And tell His glory in the coastlands".   (Isaiah 42:11-12)

זְאֵב אוֹמֵר: עַל־כָּל־דְּבַר־פֶּשַׁע עַל־שׁוֹר עַל־חֲמוֹר עַל־שֶׂה עַל־שַׂלְמָה עַל־כָּל־אֲבֵדָה אֲשֶׁר יֹאמַר כִּי־הוּא זֶה עַד הָאֱ־לֹהִים יָבֹא דְּבַר־שְׁנֵיהֶם אֲשֶׁר יַרְשִׁיעֻן אֱ־לֹהִים יְשַׁלֵּם שְׁנַיִם לְרֵעֵהוּ:   (שְׁמוֹת כ״ב, ח׳)

THE WOLF SAYS: "In every question of dishonesty whether it involves an ox, a donkey, a sheep, a garment, or anything that was [allegedly] lost of which [a witness] says, 'This is it!' the claims of both parties must be brought to the judges. The one whom the judges find guilty, must pay double restitution to his neighbor".

(SHEMOT 22:8)

שׁוּעָל אוֹמֵר: הוֹי בֹּנֶה בֵיתוֹ בְּלֹא־צֶדֶק וַעֲלִיּוֹתָיו בְּלֹא מִשְׁפָּט בְּרֵעֵהוּ יַעֲבֹד חִנָּם וּפֹעֲלוֹ לֹא יִתֶּן־לוֹ: (יִרְמְיָה כ״ב, י״ג)

THE **FOX** SAYS: "Ha! he who builds his house with unfairness And his upper chambers with injustice, Who makes his fellow man work without pay And does not give him his wages".

(JEREMIAH 22:13)

זַרְזִיר אוֹמֵר: רַנְּנוּ צַדִּיקִים בַּי־הֹוָה לַיְשָׁרִים נָאוָה תְהִלָּה: (תְּהִלִּים ל״ג, א׳)

THE **GREYHOUND** SAYS: "Sing forth, O you righteous, to the LORD; it is fit that the upright acclaim Him".

(Psalms 33:1)

חָתוּל אוֹמֵר: אֶרְדּוֹף אוֹיְבַי וְאַשִּׂיגֵם וְלֹא־אָשׁוּב עַד־כַּלּוֹתָם: (תְּהִלִּים י״ח, ל״ח)

THE **CAT** SAYS: "I pursued my enemies and overtook them; I did not turn back till I destroyed them".

(Psalms 30:2)

שְׁרָצִים אוֹמְרִים: יִשְׂמַח יִשְׂרָאֵל בְּעֹשָׂיו בְּנֵי־צִיּוֹן יָגִילוּ בְמַלְכָּם: (תְּהִלִּים קמ״ט, ב׳)

THE **INSECTS** SAY: "Let Israel rejoice in its maker; let the children of Zion exult in their king". (Psalms 149:2)

אִלִּים שֶׁבַּשְּׁרָצִים אוֹמְרִים: אֶשְׁתְּךָ | כְּגֶפֶן פֹּרִיָּה בְּיַרְכְּתֵי בֵיתֶךָ בָּנֶיךָ כִּשְׁתִלֵי זֵיתִים סָבִיב לְשֻׁלְחָנֶךָ: (תְּהִלִּים קכ״ח, ג׳)

THE **REPTILES** SAY: "Your wife shall be like a fruitful vine within your house; your sons, like olive saplings around your table". (Psalms 128:3)

נָחָשׁ אוֹמֵר: סוֹמֵךְ יְ־הֹוָה לְכָל־הַנֹּפְלִים וְזוֹקֵף לְכָל־הַכְּפוּפִים:

(תְּהִלִּים קמ״ה, י״ד)

THE **SNAKE** SAYS: The LORD supports all who stumble, and makes all who are bent stand straight.

(Psalms 145:14)

עַקְרָב אוֹמֵר: טוֹב־יְ־הֹוָה לַכֹּל וְרַחֲמָיו עַל־כָּל־מַעֲשָׂיו:

(תְּהִלִּים קמ״ה, ט׳)

THE **SCORPION** SAYS: "The LORD is good to all, and His mercy is upon all His works". (Psalms 145:9)

שַׁבְּלוּל אוֹמֵר: כְּמוֹ שַׁבְּלוּל תֶּמֶס יַהֲלֹךְ נֵפֶל אֵשֶׁת בַּל־חָזוּ שָׁמֶשׁ:

(תְּהִלִּים נ״ח, ט׳)

THE **SNAIL** SAYS: "Like a snail that melts away as it moves; like a woman's stillbirth, may they never see the sun!" (Psalms 58:9)

נְמָלָה אוֹמֶרֶת: לֵךְ־אֶל־נְמָלָה עָצֵל רְאֵה דְרָכֶיהָ וַחֲכָם: (מִשְׁלֵי ו׳, ו׳)

THE **ANT** SAYS: "Lazybones, go to the ant; Study its ways and learn". (Proverbs 6:6)

עַכְבָּר אוֹמֵר: וְאַתָּה צַדִּיק עַל כָּל־הַבָּא עָלֵינוּ כִּי־אֱמֶת עָשִׂיתָ וַאֲנַחְנוּ הִרְשָׁעְנוּ:

(נחמיה ט׳, ל״ג)

THE **MOUSE** SAYS: "Surely You are in the right with respect to all that has come upon us, for You have acted faithfully, and we have been wicked". (Nehemia 9:33)

חֻלְדָה אוֹמֶרֶת: כֹּל הַנְּשָׁמָה תְּהַלֵּל יָה הַלְלוּ־יָהּ: (תהלים ק"נ, ו')

THE RAT SAYS: "Let all that breathes praise the LORD. Hallelujah". (Psalms 150:6)

כְּלָבִים אוֹמְרִים: בֹּאוּ נִשְׁתַּחֲוֶה וְנִכְרָעָה נִבְרְכָה לִפְנֵי־יְהוָה עֹשֵׂנוּ: (תהלים צ"ה, ו').

THE DOGS SAYS: "Come, let us bow down and kneel, bend the knee before the LORD our maker". (Psalms 95:6)

In the book of Kings II, it tells how the army of SANCHERIV surrounded Jerusalem in the days of KING HEZEKIAH. 180,000 of SANCHERIV's soldiers died when they came to fight against the nation of Israel and that which caused their death was the animals' singing. As it is written, RABBI YITZCHAK NAFCHA says: "He opened their ears, and they heard the songs from the mouths of the animals, and they died" (SANHEDRIN 95b).

❚❚ It is said about KING DAVID that when he completed the book of PSALMS, he became haughty and said before The Creator of the world, 'Is there any being in the world that says song like me?' A frog appeared in front of him and said, 'do not feel so proud, my song is superior to yours for within every song that I recite there are three thousand proverbs'". (YALKUT SHIMONI, PSALMS, REMEZ 889)

❧❧ **RABBI YOCHANAN** says: What is the meaning of that which is written (PROVERBS 3:33): 'The curse of the Lord is in the house of the wicked, but He blesses the habitation of the just - מְאֵרַת יְ־הֹוָה בְּבֵית רָשָׁע וּנְוֵה צַדִּיקִים יְבָרֵךְ'?

'The curse of the Lord is in the house of the wicked - מְאֵרַת יְ־הֹוָה בְּבֵית רָשָׁע' - this refers to **PEKACH,** the son of **REMALIAH,** who would eat forty SE'AH (a measurement used in those days) of fledglings for dessert.

'And He blesses the habitation of the just - וּנְוֵה צַדִּיקִים יְבָרֵךְ' - this is a reference to **HEZEKIAH,** king of **JUDEA,** who would eat a litra of vegetables at his meal".

(SANHEDRIN 94B)

EPILOGUE

THOUGHT *before* ACTION

BERESHIT – IN THE BEGINING:

ISAIAH – THE VISION OF THE END OF DAYS:

PLANT BASED NUTRITION FOR HUMANS

One who is focused on wholesome worship of God will not allow themselves to take the easy path, but will strive for high ideals.

Rabbi Avraham Yitzchak Kook:

❚❚ We must remember that in a wholesome state, before the sin, Adam was commanded not to eat meat. Therefore we know that in the time to come, after the world is repaired, the heavens and earth will be revitalized, the nature of man and beast will change and be elevated, and then we will return to that supreme moral sensitivity, and accordingly it will be forbidden to kill animals to eat their flesh". (The vision of vegetarianism and peace).

"וְכָרַתִּי לָהֶם בְּרִית בַּיּוֹם הַהוּא עִם־חַיַּת הַשָּׂדֶה וְעִם־עוֹף הַשָּׁמַיִם וְרֶמֶשׂ הָאֲדָמָה וְקֶשֶׁת וְחֶרֶב וּמִלְחָמָה אֶשְׁבּוֹר מִן־הָאָרֶץ וְהִשְׁכַּבְתִּים לָבֶטַח".

"And I will make a covenant for them on that day with the beasts of the field and with the fowl of the sky and the creeping things of the earth; and the bow, the sword, and war I will abolish from the earth, and I will let them lie down safely". (Hoshe'a 2:20)

Radak [Rabbi David Kimchi]:

❚❚ And it was said in Isaiah's prophecy: (11:6) 'And a wolf shall live with a lamb - וְגָר זְאֵב עִם־כֶּבֶשׂ', and the whole matter is as he said there:

„וְגָר זְאֵב עִם־כֶּבֶשׂ וְנָמֵר עִם־גְּדִי יִרְבָּץ וְעֵגֶל וּכְפִיר וּמְרִיא יַחְדָּו וְנַעַר קָטֹן נֹהֵג בָּם: וּפָרָה וָדֹב תִּרְעֶינָה יַחְדָּו יִרְבְּצוּ יַלְדֵיהֶן וְאַרְיֵה כַּבָּקָר יֹאכַל־תֶּבֶן: וְשִׁעֲשַׁע יוֹנֵק עַל־חֻר פָּתֶן וְעַל מְאוּרַת צִפְעוֹנִי גָּמוּל יָדוֹ הָדָה: לֹא־יָרֵעוּ וְלֹא־יַשְׁחִיתוּ בְּכָל־הַר קָדְשִׁי כִּי־מָלְאָה הָאָרֶץ דֵּעָה אֶת־יְהֹוָה כַּמַּיִם לַיָּם מְכַסִּים".

(יְשַׁעְיָהוּ י"א, ו'-ט')

"And a wolf shall live with a lamb, and a leopard shall lie with a kid; and a calf and a lion cub and a fatling [shall lie] together, and a small child shall lead them. And a cow and a bear shall graze, together their children shall lie; and a lion, like cattle, shall eat straw. And an infant shall play over the hole of a snake and over the hole of an adder, a weaned child shall stretch forth his hand. They shall neither harm nor destroy on all My holy mount, for the land shall be full of knowledge of the Lord as water covers the sea".   (ISAIAH 11, 6-9) ❧

Summary

We

have

LEARNED

that:

The ORIGINAL WILL and INTENT in THE TORAH is PLANT-BASED NUTRITION.

....

THE TORAH is NOT COMFORTABLE AT ALL WITH THE CONSUMPTION OF MEAT, and it was allowed only after the fact of man's derelict actions, which is similar to THE TORAH's permission (DEVARIM 21:11) to take the "beautifully formed woman - אֵשֶׁת יְפַת־תֹּאַר" in war.

....

In our time, IT IS NOT A MITZVAH, NOR IS IT A JOY, TO EAT MEAT, as it was in the time of THE TEMPLE.

....

The ULTIMATE REASON for the SACRIFICES was to drive the nation of Israel away from worshipping alien GODS.

....

The WORDS of our SAGES - the **RISHONIM** and **ACHRONIM** - speaking about the NEGATIVITY OF EATING ANIMALS and PRAISING PLANT-BASED EATING.

....

The PURPOSE of the CREATION of ANIMALS is FOR THEIR OWN SAKE and not for anything else.

....

Meat, dairy, eggs and all animal-based products coming from factories, come to us by the means of VIOLATING MANY SERIOUS TORAH COMMANDMENTS, and therefore these items HAVE A STATUS OF BEING FORBIDDEN TO PURCHASE.

ELIXIR OF LIFE

IN reflecting on my way of studying the issue at hand, I wondered if my interpretation and understanding of THE TORAH is correct. As THE TORAH recommends (DEVARIM 13:15), "You shall inquire, investigate, and ask thoroughly, and, behold, it is true, the matter is certain - וְדָרַשְׁתָּ וְחָקַרְתָּ וְשָׁאַלְתָּ הֵיטֵב וְהִנֵּה אֱמֶת נָכוֹן הַדָּבָר".

I rely upon the words of our sages, CHAZAL, to determine if I have studied and understood THE TORAH in a way promoting life or alternatively promoting death.

The sages have taught us:

> 'And you shall place [VE-SAM-TEM - וְשַׂמְתֶּם] these words of Mine in your hearts - וְשַׂמְתֶּם אֶת־דְּבָרַי אֵלֶּה עַל־לְבַבְכֶם' (Devarim 11:18). Read this as though it stated 'SAM TAM', i.e., a perfect elixir. THE TORAH is compared

to an **Elixir of Life**".   (KIDDUSHIN 30B)

❙❙ The more flesh - the more worms; …the more TORAH
- the more life"   (PIRKEI AVOT 2:8)

❙❙ RABBI YEHOSHUA BEN LEVI said: What is the meaning
of that which is written (DEVARIM 4:44): 'And this is THE
TORAH which Moshe put - 'וְזֹאת הַתּוֹרָה אֲשֶׁר־שָׂם מֹשֶׁה
[PUT in hebrew is: SAM]. If one is deserving, THE TORAH
becomes a potion [POTION in hebrew is: SAM] of life
for him. If one is not deserving, THE TORAH becomes a
potion of death for him".   (BAVLI, YOMA 88B).

❙❙ RAV HANANEL BAR PAPPA said: [...] so too, matters of
TORAH have the power to kill or to grant life... and that
is what RAVA said: To those who approach it in the right
way and engage in its study with strength, good will, and
sanctity, TORAH is a potion of life, and to those who approach
it wrongly, it is a potion of death".   (BAVLI, SHABBAT 88B)

We see that THE TORAH tends towards life and not towards death;
therefore the commentaries which we have brought in this book are
appropriate and suitable to the approach of THE TORAH.

RABBI CHAYIM VITAL:

❙❙ He (THE HOLY ARI OF BLESSED MEMORY) severely warned me not to
slaughter anything, not to kill any living creature, not
even lice and fleas. My master never killed lice and fleas

or any other bug".   (Sha'ar HaGilgulim, introduction 38)

Rabbi Aharon Rote:

❝ Therefore, we were forbidden to inflict undo anguish to any living thing, and our Rabbis have said (Bava Metzia 32b) , 'Tza'ar Ba'alei Chayim is a Torah law'. And if one gives anguish to even the smallest creature for no reason, that pain goes in front of **God,** and thus Heaven forbid, a person can endanger his self".

(Shomer Emunim ["Guardian of the Faith"], Private supervision article, chapter 16)

Rabbi Saadia Gaon:

❝ I will expound again upon the merits which are impossible not to come by in this world, even if one is an apostate. They are three:

1. **Honor of father and mother,** as it says (Shemot 20:12), 'Honor your father and your mother so that your days may be lengthened' - כַּבֵּד אֶת־אָבִיךָ וְאֶת־אִמֶּךָ לְמַעַן יַאֲרִכוּן יָמֶיךָ'.

2. **The mercy upon animals,** as it says (Devarim 22:7): 'You must surely send away the mother and the offspring take for yourself, so that you will benefit and you will live long - שַׁלֵּחַ תְּשַׁלַּח אֶת־הָאֵם וְאֶת־הַבָּנִים תִּקַּח־לָךְ לְמַעַן יִיטַב לָךְ וְהַאֲרַכְתָּ יָמִים'.

3. That **his negotiation will be in faith,** as it says (Devarim 25:16): 'A fully accurate, just weight, you shall have - אֶבֶן שְׁלֵמָה וָצֶדֶק יִהְיֶה־לָּךְ'.

(Emunoth veDeoth [the Book of Beliefs and Opinions], article 5)

QUESTIONS & ANSWERS

Why has the topic of TzaꞋar BaꞋalei Chayim (causing pain to animals) become an issue of public interest recently?

IN the past we did not have industrial manufacturing, but since then things have fundamentally changed. Before the development of refrigeration, transportation and the like, people rarely ate meat. But today, with technology enabling this, the situation is greatly different. For instance, in the past:

- They WOULD NOT separate the calf from its mother right after birth;
- They DID NOT cut off the beaks of chickens;
- The chicken cages WERE NOT cramped;

- The chicks WERE NOT ground up (as is done today to all of the males in egg factories, as well as the injured chickens in the chicken meat industry);
- They DID NOT electrocute the chickens to death at 2 years of age despite the fact that they can reach an age of 15 years;
- They DID NOT inject hormones into their bodies or put hormones in their feed.

In the past there was almost no Tza'ar Ba'alei Chayim throughout the animals' lives. Animals lived many years; they were slaughtered for consumption every now and then but not more than that.

Today the industry kills animals after a very short period of their life expectancy, and their life is a terrible experience. Because of the manufacturing technology, we eat much more animal food than in the past and this is the cause of so much Tza'ar Ba'alei Chayim.

Today, as a result of genetic alterations, we actually force chickens to produce more than three hundred eggs a year. We alter their perceptions of the changing seasons by means of using great darkness and then bright lights, for the purposes of increasing egg production. This destroys the chicken's body, as it is unnatural, and winds up killing her. She loses her feathers and her overly-used intestinal tube hangs and falls out of her over-used body.

After two years in cramped containment cages, when the chickens bodies are completely exhausted and they are no longer able to produce eggs, the electrocution device arrives and electrocutes all of the chickens. Then the cycle begins again with new chickens that will experience the same sad fate.

The difference now is in the quantity that is manufactured, and this directly effects the level of Tza'ar Ba'alei Chayim. A cow in nature produces eight liters of milk a day for its calf. Today, cows in pens produce 40-70 liters of milk every day. A cow in the dairy farm will be sent to slaughter after about 5 years, although in the past a cow could live 20 years.

We abuse them so we can cheaply eat meat, diary and eggs three times a day. The reason there is not much Jewish literature about the length and quality of an animal's life is that how they lived was never an issue, because they lived well. Today, however, this is a major problem that is kept out of the public's view.

What about the consumption of organic animal products?

Even with organically raised animals there is Tza'ar Ba'alei Chayim. "Organic" simply means one is eating an animal that did not have hormones injected into it and its feed did not contain pesticides or antibiotics. This does not pertain to how this animal was treated and therefore it does not reflect upon Tza'ar Ba'alei Chayim. Those animals who were fed organically also suffer from Tza'ar Ba'alei Chayim.

Animal-based products labeled as "Free Range" are a marketing technique without supervision, and there is no way to check, as manufacturer scan use this label any way they choose. Even with "Free Range Eggs" there is TZA'AR BA'ALEI CHAYIM, and they are not what they may appear to be from their name. "Free Range" can actually just mean that the chicken cage is a few inches larger or that it has an added window. It doesn't mean that the chickens move around freely, nor are they free from the cruel practices of the industry, for example beak cutting and electrocution to name a few. The cruel practices that we mentioned before exist even in these operations.

Why did GOD receive the sacrifice of ABEL who brought from the firstborn of his flock?

THE MALBIM (RABBI MEIR LEIBUSH BEN YEHIEL MICHEL WISSER):

"God almighty does not care for meat or vegetation; He responds to the heart of a person and to their intentions. In this instance ABEL brought an offering wholeheartedly as opposed to CAIN who brought forth inferior goods. Therefore, GOD said to CAIN (BERESHIT 4:7), "If you improve - הֲלוֹא אִם־תֵּיטִיב" by which He revealed that GOD does not desire the offering, as it says (SAMUEL 1, 15:22): "Surely, obedience is better than sacrifice - הִנֵּה שְׁמֹעַ מִזֶּבַח טוֹב", but an improved actions".

(THE MALBIM on BERESHIT 4:7)

Rabbi Yosef Albo writes in Sefer Ha'Ikarim:

> "Had he offered from the fruit of a tree and not vegetation from the ground... he would not have been punished, for regarding Cain it is written (Bereshit 4:7), 'Is it not so that if you improve, you will be forgiven? If you do not improve, however, at the door sin is lying... - הֲלוֹא אִם־תֵּיטִיב שְׂאֵת וְאִם לֹא תֵיטִיב לַפֶּתַח חַטָּאת'."[13]

Noah and Our Father Abraham

One cannot learn the ideal of what is proper in our generation from the incidents with Noah and with Our Father Abraham. This was the accepted behavior in their time. We must understand that despite their great righteousness, and their being our holy fathers, and that we are but dust at their feet, we still cannot learn the correct behavior in our generation from their actions. See what Maimonides has written in The interpretation of the Mishna, Tractate Chullin, at the end of chapter 7.

Noah sacrificed because he saw the generation of the flood wildly worshipping idols since the days of Enosh, as the verse says (Bereshit 6:11), "And the land became corrupted before God - וַתִּשָּׁחֵת הָאָרֶץ לִפְנֵי הָאֱ־לֹהִים". Therefore, he brought his sacrifice to distance himself from idol worship. Similarly, this was the case with Abraham Our Father who broke statues and began to inform humanity that it was only appropriate to worship the God of the world and only fitting to

13 See the entire answer in Sefer Ha'Ikarim, third article in chapter 15.

bow and sacrifice to Him. As the verse says (BERESHIT 8:21), 'The sweet smell - רֵיחַ הַנִּיחֹחַ', and RAV ABARBANEL states in the introduction to the BOOK OF VAYIKRA, "THE TORAH speaks in a language of one who brings sacrifices".

"And he took cream and milk and the calf that he had prepared, and he placed them before his guests - וַיִּקַּח חֶמְאָה וְחָלָב וּבֶן־הַבָּקָר אֲשֶׁר עָשָׂה וַיִּתֵּן לִפְנֵיהֶם" (BERESHIT 18:8). One of the explanations is that which THE MALBIM states, that this particular calf was created through the mystical SEFER YETZIRAH, and an animal created by this means is not bound by the rules of meat. By using this answer the terminology in the text is better understood, "and the calf that he 'made' - וּבֶן־הַבָּקָר אֲשֶׁר עָשָׂה", i.e., that which ABRAHAM OUR FATHER actually created himself; thus, the rules of milk and meat do not apply to it and he was able to serve them milk with the meal.

We should note that in THE TALMUD SANHEDRIN (p. 65B) "RAV CHANINA and RAV OSHAYA would sit every SHABBAT eve and engage in the study of SEFER YETZIRAH, and a third-born calf [EGLA TILTA] would be created for them, and they would eat it in honor of SHABBAT". As a consequence, the problem of milk and meat, as well as the issue of consuming meat, do not apply to this text. As THE TALMUD notes, "here we are dealing with meat from heaven".   (SANHEDRIN 59b)

Why is there a commandment for slaughtering and what is the purpose of all the SHECHITA laws?

First of all, there is no blessing "SHEHECHEYANU" for slaughtering because we are causing harm to a creation of GOD (REMA, SHULCHAN ARUCH, YOREH DE'AH, 28:2).

We have laws regarding slaves and laws regarding the beautiful woman captive and other similar commandments, and similarly also slaughtering and its laws are given only to those who want to take a life and eat it. THE TORAH refers to them and states (DEVARIM 12:20), "If you crave to eat meat - תְאַוֶּה נַפְשְׁךָ לֶאֱכֹל בָּשָׂר", then you are obligated to slaughter properly without piercing the animal.

RABBI NAFTALI ZVI YEHUDA BERLIN:

❞ SHECHITA is a negative law which comes from bypassing a positive law i.e not to eat meat without ritual slaughter". (HA'AMEK DAVAR, DEVARIM 17:14)

RABBI TZVI PESACH FRANK:

❞ One is not obligated to slaughter; it is only when one 'craves to eat meat - כִּי־תְאַוֶּה נַפְשְׁךָ לֶאֱכֹל בָּשָׂר' (DEVARIM 12:20). [...] The blessing does not come on the act of slaughtering itself because there is no obligation to slaughter if one does not want to eat meat". (RESPONSA HAR TZVI, EVEN HA'EZER, 87)

RABBI AVRAHAM IBN EZRA:

❞ GOD did not command us that there is an obligation to slaughter; He only commanded the prohibition to eat live meat, thus the animal's blood must be spilled by slaughtering and not by any other means".

(YESOD MORA ["FOUNDATION OF AWE"], SHA'AR 2)

How does THE TORAH allow us to use the skins of animals for the writing of TORAH scrolls, Mezuzot and Tefillin?

According to the law it is permitted from the outset, to produce all of the STAM (TORAH Scrolls, TEFILLIN and MEZUZOT) products from animals who died a natural death. THE TORAH does not instruct us to kill animals for the creation of STAM products:

RABBI YOSEF KARO:

> The parchment must be [made] from the skin of a domesticated animal, wild animal, or bird which are kosher... even from a carcass ['NEVELA' - i.e. a KOSHER animal which died on it's own, without proper HALACHIC slaughtering] or a TREIF [ie. a KOSHER animal which had some mortal injury or condition]".
>
> (SHULCHAN ARUCH, ORACH CHAYIM 32:12)

What is the Jewish stance on fish regarding TZA'AR BA'ALEI CHAYIM and with regard to consuming them?

The law pertaining to fish is the same as that pertaining to meat. The essential nature of the permission to eat fish is not desired by GOD from the outset, and all of the aspects of Tza'ar Ba'alei Chayim apply to fish.

(Responsa She'elat Ya'abetz, part 1, 17)

(Rabbi Menashe Klein, Responsa Mishneh Halachot, part 6, 216)

Meat consumption by some of the great Rabbis in Israel

The general reason that our sages did not forbid "that desire" is because of human health - they figured that if they would prevent people from eating meat their bodies would become weak and they would not be able to learn Torah and repair the world. Therefore, our Scholars say (Pesachim 49b): **"An ignoramus is forbidden to eat meat"**.

Furthermore, they said that eating meat is permitted only to Torah Scholars who busy themselves with repairing the world, as the verse says:

> ❝ This is the Torah of the animal and the fowl - זֹאת תּוֹרַת הַבְּהֵמָה וְהָעוֹף" (Vayikra 11:46), intimating that those who learn Torah are permitted to eat the meat of an animal or a fowl, and those who do not learn Torah are forbidden to eat meat of an animal or a fowl". (Pesachim 49b)

The Great Men of Torah throughout all the generations knew and believed in the ideal that from the outset we do not wish for people to eat meat, and they hoped for the realization of this view. However, they knew that the people in their generation were not ready for it. And it is a rule that we do not decree a rule upon the public unless most of the population can abide by it   (MAIMONIDES, HILCHOT MAMRIM, 2:6).

This is the ruling in THE TALMUD as well:

> ❙❙It is taught in a Baraita that RABBI YISHMAEL BEN ELISHA said: From the day that THE TEMPLE was destroyed we should have decreed upon ourselves not to eat meat and not to drink wine, but the sages do not issue a decree upon the public unless a majority of the public is able to abide by it".   (BAVA BATRA, 60b)

The leaders of Israel do not separate themselves from the public so that they can continue to lead the generation. For instance, RABBI YOSEF DOV SOLOVEITCHIK did not publicize his writing on this issue in his lifetime. His writings about vegetable-based nutrition as the Jewish ideal were published only after his death. In a similar manner, RABBI TZVI YEHUDA KOOK said that his father, RABBI AVRAHAM YITZCHAK KOOK, ate a little bit of meat only on SHABBAT but preferred not to eat any meat at all, however, due to his public position, he was not able to separate himself from the community and forbid himself to have it while it was permitted to others.   (CHAI RO'I [HEBREW], [5775], PAGE 127)

What is the intent of the adage, "The end of man is death and the end of an animal is slaughter"?

This saying is not a scholarly adage, rather it is a description of reality and its source is in the words of our Scholars in Tractate BERACHOT (17a):

> ▌▌When RABBI YOCHANAN concluded studying THE BOOK OF JOB, he said the following: 'A person will ultimately die and an animal will ultimately be slaughtered, and all are destined for death. Therefore, death itself is not a cause for great anguish. Rather, happy is he who grew up in TORAH, whose labor is in TORAH, who gives pleasure to his Creator, who grew up with a good name and who took leave of the world with a good name. Such a person lived his life fully, and about him KING SOLOMON said (Ecclesiastes 7): 'A good name is better than fine oil, and one's day of death is better than his day of birth - טוֹב שֵׁם מִשֶּׁמֶן טוֹב וְיוֹם הַמָּוֶת מִיּוֹם הִוָּלְדוֹ''.

Thus, we are not dealing here with the ideal nor with the ultimate purpose of animals' existence, heaven forbid, for all will die but we do not have to slaughter them. Likewise, nowhere in THE TORAH does it tell us that this is their purpose. This is simply an adage describing reality and we should not infer from it that we are permitted to eat meat, as is the way of many people in the world who slaughter and eat animals.

Why is the land of Israel called "the land flowing with milk and honey"?

MEKHILTA OF RABBI SHIMON BAR YOCHAI:

❙❙ As for 'The land flowing with milk and honey - אֶרֶץ זָבַת חָלָב וּדְבַשׁ' (SHEMOT 3:8) RABBI ELIEZER says that 'Milk' here refers to the milk of fruit and 'Honey' refers to date's honey".

(MEKHILTA OF RABBI SHIMON BAR YOCHAI, 13)

RABBEINU BACHA'YE:

❙❙ As you have sworn to our fathers, a land flowing with milk and honey - כַּאֲשֶׁר נִשְׁבַּעְתָּ לַאֲבֹתֵינוּ אֶרֶץ זָבַת חָלָב וּדְבַשׁ" – meaning that the land will give forth tasty fruit.

(DEVARIM 26:15)

RABBI JONATHAN BEN UZZIEL:

❙❙ Flowing with milk and honey - זָבַת חָלָב וּדְבַשׁ" – Its fruits are fat like milk and sweet as honey". (DEVARIM 6:3)

RABBI ISAAC BEN MOSES ARAMA:

"A land flowing with milk and honey - אֶרֶץ זָבַת חָלָב וּדְבַשׁ – not only did He mention their gift of 'a settled land - אֶרֶץ נוֹשָׁבֶת' (SHEMOT 16:35), but an abundant land filled with a variety of fruits; because GOD provides the ultimate good".

(AKEDAT YITZCHAK [BINDING OF ISAAC], DEVARIM, SHA'AR 89)

THE HOLY ALSHEICH [RABBI MOSHE ALSHEICH]:

"GOD planned to take us out from the land of Egypt to 'a land flowing with milk and honey - אֶרֶץ זָבַת חָלָב וּדְבַשׁ', which is a land blessed with the seven species of crops".

(ALSHEICH, BAMIDBAR 20)

"A land flowing with milk and honey - אֶרֶץ זָבַת חָלָב וּדְבָשׁ –
A land whose fruits are robust and sweet". (ALSHEICH, DEVARIM 6)

The land of Israel was blessed with seven species and it was only those fruits that were brought to THE TEMPLE. Not milk of sheep nor honey were brought to THE TEMPLE.

"כִּי יְהוָה אֱ-לֹהֶיךָ מְבִיאֲךָ אֶל־אֶרֶץ טוֹבָה אֶרֶץ נַחֲלֵי מָיִם עֲיָנֹת וּתְהֹמֹת יֹצְאִים בַּבִּקְעָה וּבָהָר: אֶרֶץ חִטָּה וּשְׂעֹרָה וְגֶפֶן וּתְאֵנָה וְרִמּוֹן אֶרֶץ־זֵית שֶׁמֶן וּדְבָשׁ".

"For the Lord your God is bringing you to a good land, a land with brooks of water, fountains and depths, that emerge in valleys and mountains, a land of wheat and barley, vines and figs and pomegranates, a land of oil producing olives and honey".   (DEVARIM 8:7-8)

The honey mentioned here is date honey .Likewise, the spies returning from being in the land describe its goodness (BAMIDBAR 13:27): "It is also a land flowing with milk and honey, and this is its fruit - וְגַם זָבַת חָלָב וּדְבַשׁ הִוא וְזֶה־פִּרְיָהּ", and they brought fruit with them from the land, and not milk of sheep. The term "flowing with milk and honey - זָבַת חָלָב וּדְבָשׁ" refers to its fruit.

Even according to the opinion that says it is literally milk of sheep, it is referring to the milk in the udders of sheep, symbolizing fertility, dripping due to its abundance.

See **RASHI** who explains:

"something which extrudes without effort".   (Megillah 6a)

Rabbi Avraham Ibn Ezra:

"Why 'flowing - זָבַת'? Like one who has bodily emissions – flowing without effort".   (short commentary, Shemot 33)

Why are Meat and Fish mentioned in our Shabbat songs?

These are simply songs which were written at a time when people ate meat and therefore they were composed in this manner.

The shank bone and egg on the Seder Plate:

We are dealing here with a custom and not an obligation. Therefore, one can put two different types of cooked vegetables. The Talmud relates that Rava enhanced his Seder plate by placing spinach and rice on it:

"What are the two dishes mentioned in the Mishnah? Rav Huna says: spinach and rice. Rava wanted to beautify his Seder and placed spinach and rice on his Seder plate. Since Rav Huna said it, although he did not intend to make an exclusive statement, Rava simply wanted to do exactly what Rav Huna, his rav, had said".

(Pesachim 114b)

The head of a fish on Rosh Hashanah

We are surely not talking about a Mitzvah but rather a custom using symbols relating to the festival. The source of this custom is the expression, "may we be the head and not the tail!" The intent of this adage is that we should pursue a reasonable and rational path as it is the head with which we think, and not drag after others thoughtlessly. The source of this expression is in the Bible, "God should make you the head and not the tail and you will only be above and not below - וּנְתָנְךָ יְ־הוָֹה לְרֹאשׁ וְלֹא לְזָנָב וְהָיִיתָ רַק לְמַעְלָה וְלֹא תִהְיֶה לְמָטָּה" (Devarim 28:13). The continuation of this verse does not link God's blessing with eating any specific food but rather with fulfilling God's commandments.

On Rosh Hashanah it is also customary to eat a carrot, and additional vegetables, each with an accompanying prayer. Eating a carrot with its accompanying prayer, "may God decree upon us good decrees" is only symbolic. According to all opinions there is no hint that indeed if we eat a carrot then God will decree upon us good decrees. Likewise, so it is with all the other symbols; they are merely a custom to awaken the heart to the great day and to prayer, repentance and good deeds.

On this holiday, at a time that we ask for heavenly mercy, we must first show mercy towards all of God's creations, so let us leave the head of the fish on its body while it is still alive. There are Sephardic communities who do not eat any fish on the eve of Rosh Hashanah as the Rashbatz writes, "it is not proper to eat fish in this manner" and **THE CHIDA** and **BEN ISH CHAI** say the same. These symbols from living creatures should be replaced by vegetables; instead of the head of a fish one should place the head of any vegetable, such as a cabbage. The bee honey should be replaced by any other type of sweetener like sugar (as many Sephardic communities do) or date honey or the like. (RABBI YOM TOV TZAHALON, **RESPONSA MAHARITZ**, QUESTION 244: "ANIMAL CRUELTY TENDS EVEN TOWARDS BEES")

❙❙ The reason that meat consumption is considered 'Lust' is because when Israel is spiritually whole, they do not eat meat. As is written in the Zohar:

'**MOSHE** was greatly distressed when Israel asked him for meat. Had **MOSHE** our teacher entered into the land of Israel with them, they would not have eaten meat'.

During **MOSHE**'s life they ate the Mana which was from heaven, and for 30 days after his death they also ate the Mana, because for those 30 days his soul still clung to the children of Israel, enabling them to continue receiving the Mana. After 30 days, **MOSHE**'s soul ascended to the upper worlds and the Mana completely stopped; as the verse states (DEVARIM 12:20), '**When God expands your borders -** כִּי־יַרְחִיב יְהוָה אֱלֹהֶיךָ אֶת־גְּבוּלְךָ' [...] due to this you say, '**I will eat meat -** אֹכְלָה בָשָׂר' because you crave it'".

(RABBI YOSEF KARO, MAGGID MEISHARIM, PARASHAT EKEV)

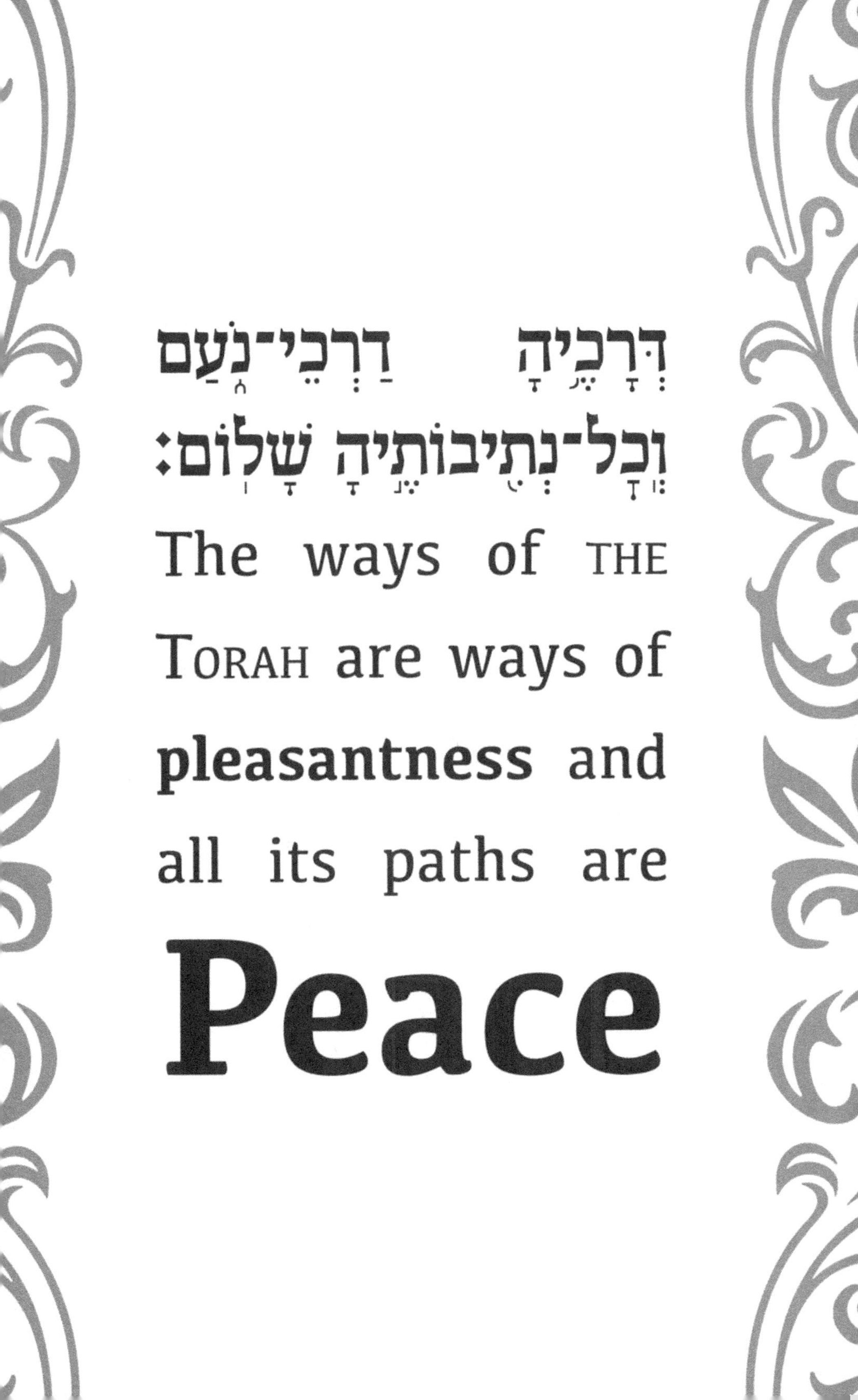

דְּרָכֶיהָ   דַּרְכֵי־נֹעַם
וְכָל־נְתִיבוֹתֶיהָ שָׁלוֹם:
The ways of THE
TORAH are ways of
pleasantness and
all its paths are
Peace

INDEX

A

Abarbanel 81–83, 92, 125–132, 165, 166, 213

Abel 125, 130, 137, 151, 152, 212

Abraham 11, 20, 42, 106, 107, 112, 130, 148, 149, 150, 155, 159, 167, 213, 214, 222

Abraham our Father 11, 150, 214

Abudraham 80

Achronim 3, 26, 31, 72, 160, 205

Adam 80, 81, 82, 96, 129, 130, 132, 164, 165, 166, 167, 202

Akedat Yitzchak 220

Alien Gods 98, 123, 124, 127, 129, 131, 155, 205

Alsheich 74, 133, 166, 220

Altars 125, 130

Amalek 104, 158, 180

Amos 140

Angel 70, 71, 142, 143, 167

Angels 144, 165

Animal 8, 10, 11, 13, 14, 16, 17, 20, 23, 24, 25, 26, 27, 29, 31, 32, 33, 35, 36, 37, 38, 39, 40, 41, 42, 43, 44, 45, 48, 49, 50, 51, 60, 61, 73, 74, 75, 76, 77, 78, 79, 80, 81, 87, 90, 97, 101, 102, 106, 107, 109, 113, 114, 119, 124, 129, 132, 134, 137, 143, 149, 150, 152, 154, 157, 159, 166, 168, 169, 171, 172, 182, 202, 205, 210, 211, 214, 215, 216, 217, 218, 219

Animal-based 23, 51, 61, 205

Animals 3, 9, 10, 12, 13, 14, 15, 16, 17, 18, 20, 24, 26, 27, 28, 32, 33, 35, 38, 40, 41, 43, 44, 45, 46, 47, 48, 50, 61, 70, 73, 74, 77, 78, 79, 80, 81, 83, 84, 88, 92, 95, 97, 101, 102, 103, 105, 112, 113, 120, 125, 127, 137, 143, 145, 146, 149, 157, 159, 160, 163, 164, 165, 166, 167, 168, 169, 171, 172, 181, 182, 183, 184, 200, 205, 208, 209, 210, 211, 216, 219

Ant 199

Api Zutri 32, 35

Ari 73, 74, 207

Aruch HaShulchan 26

Arvad 170, 171

Asa Keisar 4, 8, 10, 12, 13, 14, 15, 16, 19

Avodah Zarah 53

Avot 6, 86, 170, 184, 207

Avraham Eliyahu Harkavi 177

Azazel 157

D

E

N

S

V

W

Y

Z

www.ingramcontent.com/pod-product-compliance
Lightning Source LLC
Chambersburg PA
CBHW070751160726
48004CB00001B/148